# Eating Disorders

## About the Authors

**Stephen W. Touyz, PhD,** is Professor of Psychology and Honorary Professor of Psychological Medicine at the University of Sydney and Co-Director of the Peter Beumont Centre for Eating Disorders at Wesley Private Hospital. He has written or edited five books and over 180 research articles and book chapters on eating disorders and related topics. He is a Fellow of the Academy of Eating Disorders and the Australian Psychological Society and is Past President of the Eating Disorders Research Society. He was the inaugural treasurer of the Australian and New Zealand Academy of Eating Disorders and is an executive member of the Eating Disorder Foundation. He is a member of the Editorial Board of the European Eating Disorders Review.

**Janet Polivy, PhD,** is Professor of Psychology and Psychiatry at the University of Toronto at Mississauga. She has written or edited 4 books and over 150 research articles and book chapters on dieting, eating, and eating disorders. She is a Fellow of the Royal Society of Canada, the Association for Psychological Science, the Canadian Psychological Association, and the Society for Personality and Social Psychology, and is Treasurer of the Academy for Psychological Clinical Science.

**Phillipa Hay, MD,** is former Professor of Psychiatry and Head of Discipline of the School of Medicine, James Cook University, and Senior Consultant Psychiatrist at the Townsville Hospital. In August 2007 she took up the Foundation Chair in Mental Health at the University of Western Sydney School of Medicine. She has written over 80 research articles and book chapters on eating disorders and related topics. She is a Fellow of the Royal Australian and New Zealand College of Psychiatrists (RANZCP), Chair of the RANZCP Board of Research, Vice-President of the Australian and New Zealand Academy of Eating Disorders, and member of the Editorial Board of the International Journal of Eating Disorders, the Academy of Eating Disorders, and the Board of Examiners of the Australian Medical Council.

## Advances in Psychotherapy – Evidence-Based Practice

The basic objective of this series is to provide therapists with practical, evidence-based treatment guidance for the most common disorders seen in clinical practice – and to do so in a "reader-friendly" manner. Each book in the series is both a compact "how-to-do" reference on a particular disorder for use by professional clinicians in their daily work, as well as an ideal educational resource for students and for practice-oriented continuing education.
The most important feature of the books is that they are practical and "reader-friendly:" All are structured similarly and all provide a compact and easy-to-follow guide to all aspects that are relevant in real-life practice. Tables, boxed clinical "pearls", marginal notes, and summary boxes assist orientation, while checklists provide tools for use in daily practice.

# Eating Disorders

**Stephen W. Touyz**
School of Psychology, University of Sydney, Australia

**Janet Polivy**
Department of Psychology, University of Toronto, Canada

**Phillipa Hay**
School of Medicine, University of Western Sydney, Australia

**Library of Congress Cataloging in Publication**

is available via the Library of Congress Marc Database under the
LC Control Number 2008921333


**Library and Archives Canada Cataloguing in Publication**

Touyz, S. W. (Stephen W.)
   Eating disorders / Stephen W. Touyz, Janet Polivy, Phillipa Hay.

(Advances in psychotherapy--evidence-based practice)
Includes bibliographical references.
ISBN 978-0-88937-318-1

   1. Eating disorders.  2. Eating disorders--Treatment.
I. Polivy, Janet  II. Hay, Phillipa  III. Title.  IV. Series.

RC552.E18T69 2008          616.85'26          C2008-900543-0




© 2008 by Hogrefe & Huber Publishers

PUBLISHING OFFICES
USA:          Hogrefe & Huber Publishers, 875 Massachusetts Avenue, 7th Floor,
              Cambridge, MA 02139
              Phone (866) 823-4726, Fax (617) 354-6875; E-mail info@hhpub.com
EUROPE:       Hogrefe & Huber Publishers, Rohnsweg 25, 37085 Göttingen, Germany
              Phone +49 551 49609-0, Fax +49 551 49609-88, E-mail hh@hhpub.com

SALES & DISTRIBUTION
USA:          Hogrefe & Huber Publishers, Customer Services Department,
              30 Amberwood Parkway, Ashland, OH 44805
              Phone (800) 228-3749, Fax (419) 281-6883, E-mail custserv@hhpub.com
EUROPE:       Hogrefe & Huber Publishers, Rohnsweg 25, 37085 Göttingen, Germany
              Phone +49 551 49609-0, Fax +49 551 49609-88, E-mail hh@hhpub.com

OTHER OFFICES
CANADA:       Hogrefe & Huber Publishers, 1543 Bayview Avenue, Toronto, Ontario M4G 3B5
SWITZERLAND:  Hogrefe & Huber Publishers, Länggass-Strasse 76, CH-3000 Bern 9

Hogrefe & Huber Publishers
Incorporated and registered in the State of Washington, USA, and in Göttingen, Lower Saxony,
Germany

Printed and bound in the USA
ISBN  978-0-88937-318-1

# Preface

This book describes the well-known eating disorders comprising anorexia nervosa (AN), bulimia nervosa (BN), eating disorders not otherwise specified (EDNOS), and binge eating disorder (BED). Despite the serious nature of eating disorders, and AN in particular (which has the highest mortality rate of all psychiatric disorders), the development of clinically effective treatments that would prove to be successful in the majority of our patients remains elusive. Yet each day, in consulting rooms in hospitals, clinics, and private practice, patients afflicted with an eating disorder turn to therapists to provide them with treatment to alleviate their suffering. And despite the ego-syntonic nature of AN, patients suffer an ever decreasing quality of life. Even those clinicians who have a special expertise in the treatment of eating disorders find themselves in despair trying to persuade a seriously ill patient to accept treatment with absolutely no success.

This is where this book can help. It builds on existing knowledge as well as the enormous wealth of clinical experience that the authors have developed over the past three decades. It assumes a basic understanding of therapeutic intervention and some clinical training. This book will be of interest, not only to those clinicians who have developed a special expertise in eating disorders, but to psychologists, psychiatrists, general practitioners, dietitians, social workers, nurses, and other allied mental health practitioners as well.

The book is divided into five chapters. The first chapter describes the different eating disorders (AN, BN, EDNOS, and BED) and then sets out to show how they are defined and diagnosed. Empirically supported diagnostic and assessment techniques are then reviewed. Chapter 2 explores the theoretical models which underpinning the development and maintenance of eating disorders and their implications for treatment. In Chapter 3, practical strategies are provided to facilitate undertaking the initial interviews and to ensure that the appropriate medical assessment and laboratory investigations have been done. Chapter 4 provides a detailed practical account using in-session dialogs and didactic pearls to illustrate as clearly as possible the psychological techniques and interventions available to the clinician. Potential obstacles to treatment, especially with the poorly motivated and uncooperative patients are given special attention. Finally, Chapter 5 includes a series of case examples which illustrate the complexities of these disorders and the obstacles to successful treatment. The appendices provide handouts and additional information to use in treatment sessions.

Eating disorders remain an interesting challenge for clinicians. Because these disorders are heterogeneous in nature, one treatment does not fit all. As a result, this book has not been written as a "cookbook" or manual but rather as a practical guide so that the clinician can better tailor the treatment to the needs of each particular patient. It also provides helpful strategies and clinical pearls to assist the clinician especially at those difficult moments when confronted by a recalcitrant patient. There is much didactic material that can be shared with patients and when all else seems lost, some humor to keep the ship afloat.

# Acknowledgments

We are indebted to a large number of people who have contributed in their own special way to the success of this book. These include editors Danny Wedding and Linda Carter Sobell, and Robert Dimbleby of Hogrefe and Huber Publishers, whose guidance and support was invaluable and very much appreciated. We are also indebted to the late Peter Beumont, not only for his innovation in clinical practice, but for his determination to leave no stone unturned in the quest to alleviate the suffering for those with an eating disorder.

This book is dedicated to all our patients, both past and present from whom we have learnt so much. They have challenged us and, unfortunately, at times found us wanting, but this has inspired us to continue our search to better understand and to find new ways to treat these debilitating disorders.

We are very grateful to our wonderful colleague and friend, Peter Herman, for his invaluable encouragement and support throughout this endeavor and for his special brand of humor which got us through the difficult times.

The objective of this new series is to provide clinicians with practical evidence-based treatments for the most common disorders in clinical practice but written in a reader friendly and practical manner. To this end, we would like to thank Jonathan S. Abramowitz for setting the benchmark in this series and for future books such as ours. We would also like to thank Christopher Fairburn for the up to date information regarding the publication of his EDE-Q6. To Cindy Li, who despite her onerous workload, found the time to type drafts and format figures, our much appreciated gratitude. A special word of thanks to Ethel Harris, Eva Naumann, and Alex Blaszczynski for their contribution to formatting the diagrams and to Belinda Ingram for her assistance with the final draft.

Finally to our families, for their enduring love, patience, encouragement, and affection.

# Dedication

To Wren and our children, Justin and Lauren, for their enduring love and affection and to my mentor, colleague, and friend, the late Peter Beumont for his inspiration and wisdom.
　　SWT

To Peter, Lisa/Leah, Eric, and Saretta for all they are to me and to Dick Bootzin and Ken Howard for all they did to help me to become a psychologist and therapist.
　　JP

To Anne Hall who provided inspiration and superb mentoring in my "salad days," and to Kevin and Beatrix for their enduring love and patience.
　　PH

# Table of Contents

Because the greater majority of patients who have eating disorders are female, we have used feminine nouns and pronouns throughout this book.

# 1

# Description

## 1.1    Terminology

The first documented eating disorder (ED) was anorexia nervosa (AN), which was described in the medical literature in 1874. In the 1970s AN was subtyped into those who simply restricted and exercised (anorexia nervosa – restricting type) and those who purged, some of whom also binge ate (anorexia nervosa – purging type). This latter type of AN was identified as a separate disorder in normal weight women in 1979 and named bulimia nervosa (BN). It later became apparent that not all patients met the full criteria for either AN or BN, but seemed nonetheless to have more than simply a subthreshold version of the disorder. These patients were grouped together into the category of eating disorder not otherwise specified (EDNOS) in DSM-III-R in 1987 (American Psychiatric Association, 1987). A subtype of EDNOS that has received a lot of attention because it is more common, especially among obese individuals, is binge eating disorder (BED) wherein individuals binge eat but do not purge the excess food.

## 1.2    Definitions

Fairburn and Walsh (2002) defined an eating disorder as "a persistent disturbance of eating behavior or behavior intended to control weight, which significantly impairs physical health or psychosocial functioning. This disturbance should not be secondary to any recognized general medical disorder...or any

---

**Clinical Vignette**

**Different Eating Disorders**

What do a 12-year-old girl who refuses to eat more than a minute amount of vegetables each day, and who weighs less than 85% of what her peers weigh, and a 21-year-old woman who gorges herself with cake, cookies, and junk food three nights a week and then forces herself to vomit have in common? Both would be diagnosed as having an eating disorder. Eating disorders have become increasingly prevalent recently in Westernized societies, possibly due, at least in part, to periods of relative affluence and enhanced social opportunities for women (Bemporad, 1997). In fact, however, the sorts of voluntary self-starvation and episodes of binge eating and purging that characterize eating disorders have been reported throughout history.

other psychiatric disorder" (page 171). In this book, we will discuss the major recognized eating disorders, using the *Diagnostic and Statistical Manual of Mental Disorders*, 4th Edition, Text Revision (DSM-IV-TR; American Psychiatric Association, 2000a) and the *International Statistical Classification of Diseases and Related Health Problems*, 10th Edition (ICD-10; World Health Organization, 1992) to describe the primary features of anorexia nervosa (AN), bulimia nervosa (BN), and atypical eating disorders, or eating disorder not otherwise specified (EDNOS), a somewhat controversial category described by some as a catchall or residual group of subthreshold disorders, whose sufferers do not quite meet the criteria for AN or BN (Williamson et al., 2002), or by others as a set of distinct, long-lasting, and debilitating disorders rather than as simply subthreshold versions of AN or BN (Fairburn & Bohn 2005, Fairburn & Harrison, 2003). The DSM-IV-TR reflects the North American standard criteria for defining eating disorders, and in Europe the criteria detailed in the ICD-10 predominate. It should be noted, that the questions of whether to divide the eating disorders into separate diagnoses and exactly how to separate them are both still controversial (Fairburn, Cooper, & Shafran, 2003; Polivy & Herman, 2002), but we will maintain the usual diagnostic conventions for the purposes of this book.

**Diagnostic criteria for eating disorders**

To establish the DSM-IV-TR criteria for eating disorders, empirically validated symptoms were compiled by a panel of experts, and refined further by others in the field. The ICD-10 operationalizes the eating disorders in a similar manner to the DSM-IV-TR. Not all criteria for the disorders are easy to define (e.g., exactly what behaviors constitute binge eating? How much food comprises a binge?), and there is a lack of consensus on some symptoms (such as the requirement of amenorrhea for AN); the criteria as listed thus have some ambiguities. The categorical nature of these classificatory systems has been questioned (e.g., Williamson, Gleaves, & Stewart 2005), given the shifts in both criteria and the categories themselves over time. Moreover, the two sets of criteria are only moderately concordant in some areas because of different symptom criteria and thresholds for diagnoses (Ottosson, Ekselius, Grann, & Kullgren, 2002). Despite these ambiguities in the criteria, the two diagnostic systems help to point to symptoms that need to be treated, methods of treating them, and also allow for assessment of successful change, and thus they remain the standard for diagnosing the disorders.

Finally, the use of these diagnostic criteria is not encouraged for children younger than age 10 (who do not usually present with traditional eating disorders), as they have not been found to be reliable for diagnosing the eating problems of younger children (Nichols, Chater, & Lask, 2000), despite the fact that children as young as 8 are now presenting with eating disorders (Watkins & Lask, 2002).

### 1.2.1    Anorexia Nervosa (AN)

The key criteria for the diagnosis of AN are: (a) Weight loss and/or maintenance of a weight at least 15% below what is normal for height (and age); (b) Intense fear of becoming fat (DSM-IV-TR) or self-infliction of reduced weight by avoidance of "fattening foods" (ICD-10); (c) Disturbed or distorted

**Table 1**
**DSM IV-TR Diagnostic Criteria for 307.1 Anorexia Nervosa**

A. Refusal to maintain body weight at or above a minimally normal weight for age and height (e.g., weight loss leading to maintenance of body weight less than 85% of that expected; or failure to make expected weight gain during period of growth, leading to body weight less than 85% of that expected).

B. Intense fear of gaining weight or becoming fat, even though underweight.

C. Disturbance in the way in which one's body weight or shape is experienced, undue influence of body weight or shape on self-evaluation, or denial of the seriousness of the current low body weight.

D. In postmenarcheal females, amenorrhea, the absence of at least three consecutive menstrual cycles. (A woman is considered to have amenorrhea if her periods occur only following hormone, e.g., estrogen, administration.)

*Specify type:*

Restricting Type:

   During the current episode of anorexia nervosa, the person has not regularly engaged in binge-eating or purging behavior (i.e., self-induced vomiting or the misuse of laxatives, diuretics, or enemas).

Binge-Eating/Purging Type:

   During the current episode of anorexia nervosa, the person has regularly engaged in binge-eating or purging behavior (i.e., self-induced vomiting or the misuse of laxatives, diuretics, or enemas).

Reprinted with permission from the *Diagnostic and Statistical Manual of Mental Disorders, Fourth Edition, Text Revision* (© 2000), American Psychiatric Association.

**Table 2**
**ICD-10 Diagnostic Criteria for Anorexia Nervosa**

A. There is weight loss or, in children, a lack of weight gain, leading to a body weight at least 15% below the normal or expected weight for age and height.

B. The weight loss is self-induced by avoidance of "fattening foods."

C. There is self-perception of being too fat, with an intrusive dread of fatness, which leads to a self-imposed low weight threshold.

D. A widespread endocrine disorder involving the hypothalamic-pituitary-gonadal axis is manifested in women as amenorrhea and in men as a loss of sexual interest and potency. (An apparent exception is the persistence of vaginal bleeds in anorexic women who are on replacement hormonal therapy, most commonly taken as a contraceptive pill).

E. The disorder does not meet the criteria A and B for bulimia nervosa (F50.2)

World Health Organization (1992). *International statistical classification of diseases and related problems* (10th rev.). Geneva: Author.

perception of one's body, which is seen as too fat despite the emaciation; (d) Amenorrhea in postmenarcheal females (DSM-IV-TR) or hypothalamic-pituitary-gonadal endocrine disorder leading to amenorrhea in females and loss of sexual interest or potency in males (ICD-10). In addition, the DSM-IV-TR specifies either *restricting type* (no regular incidents of binge eating or purging) or *binge-eating/purging type* (regular episodes of binge eating and/or purging behavior occur during the current anorexic episode), while ICD-10 requires that the disorder not meet the first two criteria for BN.

**Two types of AN: those who do and those who do not binge/purge**

Two subtypes are generally distinguished in AN (as in the DSM-IV-TR diagnostic criteria): those who do and those who do not engage in binge eating and/or purging behaviors. Those who binge and purge seem to differ on a variety of dimensions from those who merely restrict, ranging from premorbid differences, such as higher childhood weight and more familial obesity, to personality differences such as borderline, narcissistic, or antisocial personality traits, to behavioral differences including impulsive behaviors such as stealing (food, in many cases), alcohol or drug abuse, and self-mutilating behavior (e.g., Garfinkel, 2002). The purging form of AN seems to be associated with a worse prognosis (Beumont, 2002).

**Associated features include affective and behavioral problems**

Associated features described in the DSM-IV-TR include depressed mood, social withdrawal, insomnia, and decreased sex drive; all of these appear to be secondary to the severe caloric restriction resulting in semistarvation. In addition, obsessive-compulsive behaviors (not necessarily food-related) are also common, though these, too, may reflect malnutrition. Feelings of ineffectiveness and a need for control over aspects of one's environment are psychological issues that seem to be unique to AN (APA, 2000b), and perfectionism is widely recognized as a feature in these patients (Jacobi, Hayward, de Zwaan, Kraemer, & Agras, 2004). Patients with the binge/purge subtype of AN also display more impulsive behaviors, such as drug or alcohol abuse, sexual acting out, and unstable moods.

Physically, in addition to the extreme thinness or emaciation characterizing the disorder, endocrine (estrogen) disturbances as manifested in amenorrhea (as in the DSM-IV-TR criteria), as well as a variety of blood, chemical, cardiac, EEG, and physical symptoms of starvation may be present (APA, 2000b). A hypothalamic-gonadal-pituitary endocrine disorder (as in the ICD-10 criteria) also may appear, often before any significant weight loss has occurred.

**Where is the border between disordered eating and eating disorder?**

The exaggerated desire for thinness, described by Bruch decades ago as "relentless" (e.g., Bruch, 1973), has long been recognized as a primary psychological feature of AN, but it is often difficult to distinguish this "phobic" avoidance of fatness from the "normal" pursuit of thinness by young female dieters (Polivy & Herman, 1987). Thus, it is generally not possible to diagnose AN until it is so severe that weight has declined markedly, and has progressed well beyond normal to a seriously pathological level. Once the disorder becomes established, and weight loss progresses in this manner, AN becomes self-perpetuating, as the effects of semistarvation begin to influence affect and cognition (Beumont & Touyz, 2003). Psychologically, this is manifested as both fear of fatness and a tendency to base one's self-worth on body shape and weight (McFarlane, McCabe, Jarry, Olmsted, & Polivy, 2001).

**Patients often exercise compulsively**

While it is not part of the diagnostic criteria, it is well known that these patients often exercise excessively, in a compulsive manner, insisting on exercising even

---

**Clinical Pearl**
**Early Warning Signs**

---

An early clue to the possible development of AN occurs when the patient's dieting becomes so rigid and inflexible that she won't eat or attend a special family function (e.g., a birthday) or go on a holiday because she may not find any suitable food to eat. At this point the patient has crossed the boundary from strict dieting to a possible pathological eating disorder.

when hospitalized and on bed rest (Beumont, Arthur, Russell, & Touyz 1994). Anxiety and food restriction have been found to contribute to this compulsive exercising (Holtkamp, Hedebrand, & Herpertz-Dahlman, 2004). Moreover, the deliberate exercising done to produce weight loss is only one form of hyperactivity observed in these patients. Late in the illness, many develop a persistent restlessness and sleep disturbance that is beyond their conscious control (Beumont, 2002). This appears to resemble the sort of overactivity observed in food-deprived laboratory animals, and may reflect decreased core body temperature.

Similarly, no mention is made in either the DSM-IV-TR or the ICD-10 of bizarre eating behaviors that seem to characterize AN. For example, patients often cut their food into tiny pieces, which they then move around the plate as they eat painfully slowly; in addition, they secretly dispose of food (into napkins, pockets, or other receptacles), and avoid many foods that they consider to be "dangerous" (read "fattening"). **Bizarre eating behaviors characterize AN**

As mentioned earlier, there is some controversy around some of the criteria required for a diagnosis of AN. Women with all the symptoms except amenorrhea seem to be as pathologic on every other dimension as are those with amenorrhea, so it is not clear that amenorrhea should be included as a requisite symptom for AN (Garfinkel, 2002). The weight threshold for the diagnosis is also subject to debate.

## 1.2.2    Bulimia Nervosa (BN)

As for AN, there is a reasonable degree of overlap between the two main classificatory systems for the diagnosis of BN. The diagnostic criteria are: (a) Both the DSM-IV-TR and the ICD-10 begin with the presence of recurrent episodes of overeating or eating binges that occur at least twice weekly and have persisted for at least 3 months; (b) Both systems also require the occurrence of compensatory behavior to prevent weight gain from the calories ingested in the binge eating (by one or more of self-induced vomiting, use of laxatives, diuretics, enemas, or other purgatives or medications, periods of fasting or starvation); and (c) Self-evaluation is based excessively on weight and shape (DSM-IV-TR) or one feels too fat or fears fatness (ICD-10).

The DSM-IV-TR goes on to attempt to define binge eating, indicating that the amount eaten must be greater than what most people would eat in a similar period of time, and that there must be a feeling of loss of control over eating associated with the episode, whereas the ICD-10 merely requires that the overeating involve large amounts of food eaten in short periods of time. The DSM- **Defining binge eating**

**Table 3**
**DSM-IV-TR Diagnostic Criteria for 307.51 Bulimia Nervosa**

A. Recurrent episodes of binge eating. An episode of binge eating is characterized by both of the following:
   1. Eating, in a discrete period of time (e.g., within any 2-hour period), an amount of food that is definitely larger than most people would eat during a similar period of time and under similar circumstances
   2. A sense of lack of control over eating during the episode (e.g., a feeling that one cannot stop eating or control what or how much one is eating)

B. Recurrent inappropriate compensatory behavior in order to prevent weight gain, such as self-induced vomiting; misuse of laxatives, diuretics, enemas, or other medications; fasting; or excessive exercise.

C. The binge eating and inappropriate compensatory behaviors both occur, on average, at least twice a week for 3 months.

D. Self-evaluation is unduly influenced by body shape and weight.

E. The disturbance does not occur exclusively during episodes of anorexia nervosa.

*Specify type:*

Purging Type:
   During the current episode of bulimia nervosa, the person has regularly engaged in self-induced vomiting or the misuse of laxatives, diuretics, or enemas

Nonpurging Type:
   During the current episode of bulimia nervosa, the person has used other inappropriate compensatory behaviors, such as fasting or excessive exercise, but has not regularly engaged in self-induced vomiting or the misuse of laxatives, diuretics, or enemas.

Reprinted with the permission from the *Diagnostic and Statistical Manual of Mental Disorders, Fourth Edition, Text Revision* (© 2000), American Psychiatric Association.

**Table 4**
**ICD-10 Diagnostic Criteria for Bulimia Nervosa**

A. There are recurrent episodes of overeating (at least twice a week over a period of 3 months) in which large amounts of food are consumed in short periods of time.

B. There is a persistent preoccupation with eating, and a strong desire or a sense of compulsion to eat (craving).

C. The patient attempts to counteract the "fattening" effects of food by one or more of the following:
   1. Self-induced vomiting.
   2. Self-induced purging.
   3. Alternative periods of starvation.
   4. Use of drugs such as appetite suppressants, thyroid preparations, or diuretics; when bulimia occurs in diabetic patients they may choose to neglect their insulin treatment.

D. There is self-perception of being too fat, with an intrusive dread of fatness (usually leading to underweight).

World Health Organization (1992). *International statistical classification of diseases and related problems* (10th rev.). Geneva: Author.

IV-TR mentions that the binge eating is generally done in secrecy, and may be triggered by stress or dysphoria. In addition, the DSM-IV-TR divides BN into purging and nonpurging types, depending on how the person compensates for the eating binges, and specifies that the binge/purge behaviors do not occur during episodes of AN (APA, 2000b). The ICD-10 criteria add the presence of craving or feelings of compulsion to eat as an additional factor.

**There are two types of BN: purging and nonpurging**

The purging patients exhibit more psychopathology than do the nonpurgers, including increased disturbance in body image and weight concerns, anxiety about eating/gaining weight, self-injury, and comorbidity with other disorders (Garfinkel, 2002). Mood disturbances are common in both subtypes of BN, though depression and anxiety may be results of bingeing and purging rather than preceding factors. BN patients tend to be normal weight, though there is some indication that premorbid overweight or obesity is common.

Physically, repeated purging may cause electrolyte imbalances, metabolic problems, dental problems, enlarged parotid glands, and even cardiac disorders (from repeated use of ipecac to induce vomiting).

---

**Clinical Pearl**
**Medical Complications**

The clinician should never underestimate the risk of medical complications of BN, despite apparent normal weight. Potential medical problems, such as electrolyte imbalance from repeated purging, to actual damage to heart muscle and other organs should be investigated by a full medical evaluation/examination and appropriate laboratory investigations.

---

Psychologically, BN patients tend to be impulsive, acting out sexually, stealing, and intentionally injuring themselves (Polivy & Herman, 2002). Binges tend to be planned in advance: specific "binge" foods are purchased (often foods that are both easy to swallow and fattening, or foods that the patient normally avoids eating when not bingeing). In addition, BN patients who are bingeing generally eat very quickly, stuffing the food into their mouths without even tasting it. Some patients chew the food and spit it out, but most regurgitate (often drinking large quantities of water with the food to facilitate this), or abuse laxatives or diuretics to induce diarrhea or lose fluids. Binge eating is generally done in secret when the patient is alone, although groups of girls have been known to binge together and emulate each other's binge eating behavior (Crandall, 1988).

**BN patients tend to be impulsive**

There are questions about the appropriateness of the criteria for BN, in particular the arbitrary cut-off of two binges per week. There is little or no evidence demonstrating that bingeing twice a week is more pathological than bingeing once a week (Garfinkel, 2002). Excessive exercising is mentioned in the DSM-IV-TR criteria as a possible compensatory behavior in BN, but recent research indicates that it may be more the compulsive nature of the exercising that is pathological than its mere quantity (Adkins & Peel, 2005). Finally, the definition of what constitutes a binge is particularly vexed, as there are both objective (amount of food in a particular period of time) and subjective elements (feeling out of control of one's eating). If only one of these is present (e.g., eating an apple, but feeling out of control, and thus calling it a binge), this is not strictly a binge, but it is still problematic. In particular, such "subjective bingeing" is often seen in AN where there is a distorted perception of food size. (Polivy & Herman, 2002; see also Section 1.7.3).

### 1.2.3    Eating Disorder Not Otherwise Specified (EDNOS) or Atypical Eating Disorder

AN and BN are what most people think of as eating disorders. In fact, as many as 30–60% of eating disorder patients do not meet the criteria for either AN or BN, but fall into a category of "atypical" eating disorders known as eating disorders not otherwise specified, or EDNOS (Fairburn & Walsh, 2002).

**Atypical eating disorders do not meet the criteria for AN or BN, but have features of one or both disorders**

The DSM-IV-TR criteria for EDNOS and the ICD-10 criteria for atypical eating disorders both specify that these are eating disorders that do not quite meet the criteria for AN or BN, but have features of one or both. DSM-IV-TR gives examples such as meeting all the criteria for AN except for amenorrhea or weight below 85% of normal, or meeting the BN criteria except for frequency or duration of binge/purge episodes, or inappropriate eating (e.g., binge eating disorder (BED), consisting of recurrent binge episodes, but no compensatory behavior) or inappropriate compensatory behavior (e.g., vomiting after small amounts of food, chewing food but spitting it out without swallowing) (APA, 2000b). The ICD-10 actually utilizes specific codes for each of six atypical eating disorder diagnoses (atypical AN, wherein all but one or two key features of AN are present; atypical BN, wherein all but one or two key features of BN are present; overeating associated with other psychological disturbances, including psychogenic overeating; vomiting associated with other psychological disturbances, wherein repeated vomiting occurs for psychological reasons; other eating disorders, including pica; and eating disorder, unspecified (WHO, 1992).

**Table 5**
**307.50 DSM-IV-TR Eating Disorder Not Otherwise Specified**

The eating disorder not otherwise specified category is for disorders of eating that do not meet the criteria for any specific eating disorder. Examples include:

1. For females, all of the criteria for anorexia nervosa are met except that the individual has regular menses.
2. All of the criteria for anorexia nervosa are met except that, despite significant weight loss, the individual's current weight is in the normal range.
3. All of the criteria for bulimia nervosa are met except that the binge eating and inappropriate compensatory mechanisms occur at a frequency of less than twice a week or for a duration of less than 3 months.
4. The regular use of inappropriate compensatory behavior by an individual of normal body weight after eating small amounts of food (e.g., self-induced vomiting after the consumption of two cookies).
5. Repeatedly chewing and spitting out, but not swallowing, large amounts of food.
6. Binge-eating disorder: Recurrent episodes of binge eating in the absence of the regular use of inappropriate compensatory behaviors characteristic of bulimia nervosa.

Reprinted with the permission from the *Diagnostic and Statistical Manual of Mental Disorders, Fourth Edition, Text Revision* (© 2000), American Psychiatric Association.

---

**Table 6**
**DSM-IV-TR Research Criteria for Binge-Eating Disorder**

A. Recurrent episodes of binge eating. An episode of binge eating is characterized by both of the following:

1. Eating, in a discrete period of time (e.g., within any 2-hour period), an amount of food that is definitely larger than most people would eat during a similar period of time and under similar circumstances.

2. A sense of lack of control over eating during the episode (e.g., a feeling that one cannot stop eating or control what or how much one is eating).

B. The binge-eating episodes are associated with three (or more) of the following:
   1. Eating much more rapidly than normal.
   2. Eating until feeling uncomfortably full.
   3. Eating large amounts of food when not feeling physically hungry.
   4. Eating alone because of being embarrassed by how much one is eating.
   5. Feeling disgusted with oneself, depressed, or very guilty after overeating.

C. Marked distress regarding binge eating is present.

D. The binge eating occurs, on average, at least 2 days a week for 6 months.

   *Note:* The method of determining frequency differs from that used for bulimia nervosa; future research should address whether the preferred method of setting a frequency threshold is counting the number of days on which binges occur or counting the number of episodes of binge eating.

E. The binge eating is not associated with the regular use of inappropriate compensatory behaviors (e.g., purging, fasting, excessive exercise) and does not occur exclusively during the course of anorexia nervosa or bulimia nervosa.

Reprinted with the permission from the *Diagnostic and Statistical Manual of Mental Disorders, Fourth Edition, Text Revision* (© 2000), American Psychiatric Association.

---

In both sets of criteria, there appear to be disorders similar to AN and BN, but not quite meeting one or more of the diagnostic criteria, plus disorders such as BED and pica that differ more markedly from AN and BN. Statistical attempts to subclassify the disorders lumped together into the EDNOS category have not succeeded, and problems have frequently been noted between the boundaries for the two subtypes of BN and BED (Fairburn & Walsh, 2002).

There have been objections to the use of EDNOS as a diagnostic category, and more specifically to the subheading of BED in the DSM-IV-TR. For example, Cooper and Fairburn (2003) point out that many patients categorized as BED actually have BN, and many others have no real disorder, but are obese individuals who sometimes overeat. Moreover, Beumont and Touyz (2003) point out that, other than for BED, the lack of consistency in pathology and psychopathology for EDNOS patients argues against EDNOS as a clinical entity.

## 1.3    Epidemiology

Eating disorders occur most often in adolescent females and young women living in industrialized countries. Community and clinical epidemiological

**ED predominantly occurs in young females in industrialized countries**

studies consistently find a sex ratio of one male patient to 10–15 females (except in preadolescents, where the sex ratio is closer to equal). AN occurs most often in pubertal girls, whereas BN develops slightly later, in somewhat older teenaged girls or young women in their twenties (Polivy, Herman, Mills, & Wheeler, 2003). The distribution of EDNOS is less well-studied, despite its greater prevalence. For example, at an eating disorders clinic in the UK, of 200 participants, 190 exhibited a clinical eating disorder, and among these, 11 patients met criteria for AN, 45 for BN, and the remaining 134 were diagnosed with EDNOS (Turner & Bryant-Waugh, 2004). Other estimates indicate that approximately half of patients seeking treatment for eating disorders have atypical variants or EDNOS (Fairburn & Walsh, 2002).

Looking at prevalence (number of cases in a population at a given time) and incidence rates (number of new cases in a population in a given year), it appears that the prevalence of AN and BN combined in the population at risk (young females) is somewhere between 1.5–10%, with at least a 2:1 ratio of BN to AN patients (Polivy & Herman, 2002), though more rigorous recent studies suggest the lower number is more accurate (Hoek, 2002). Moreover, the prevalence of atypical disorders or EDNOS is as much as twice that of AN and BN (Polivy & Herman, 2002).

Incidence rates of such rare disorders cannot really be based on general population studies, but instead are based on cases reported to health care systems (which are thus underestimates of the true incidence, as eating disorder patients often do not seek medical attention). Such incidence data as do exist, however, seem to indicate that the rate of AN is around 5–8 per 100,000 people per year, and for BN is closer to 11–13.5 per 100,000 (Hoek, 2002).

## 1.4    Course and Prognosis

**Initially eating disorders may look like normal dieting**

Eating disorders generally begin with what may look like normal dieting. For AN patients, eating is restricted more and more, in the "relentless" pursuit of thinness (which is never quite felt to have been achieved, no matter how emaciated the AN patient becomes). The initial desire to lose weight and become slimmer is soon replaced by more bizarre cognitions about being unworthy of food, needing to punish oneself with unremitting exercise, and needing to be thinner and eat less than anyone else. Being emaciated becomes the ultimate goal, rather than being a means for becoming happier, and the AN patient is filled with self-loathing and guilt if she gives in to her hunger and eats.

Similarly, in BN, dieting generally comes first, only later to be followed by eating binges and compensatory behaviors to get rid of the food. There is a small subgroup of patients who do not begin by dieting, but just start bingeing (fewer than 20%), but they do not differ greatly from other bulimic patients (Bulik, Sullivan, Carter, & Joyce, 1997). The attempts to restrict caloric intake eventually give way to episodes of binge eating and the development of compensatory behaviors such as vomiting or laxative abuse to eliminate the unwanted food. Patients often feel pleased with themselves in the early stages of the disorder, believing that they have found the secret to eating all they want without gaining weight. However, this initial elation is soon replaced by distress about the binge/purge behaviors, and a realization that one is not in control of them.

Over time, the relationship between typical and atypical eating disorders seems to change frequently, with both AN and BN often subsiding into a "subthreshold" phase of continued disordered eating that does not meet criteria for either AN or BN, but may still qualify as EDNOS or atypical eating disorder (Fairburn & Walsh, 2002). Approximately one third of patients continue to exhibit full clinical syndromes for 5 years or more after initial diagnosis (even with treatment), but more than 50% do show major signs of improvement in this time period (Polivy & Herman 2002). AN in particular has an exceptionally high mortality rate, though, and is possibly the most lethal of the psychological disorders (Beumont & Touyz, 2003). In addition to the dangers from complications due to malnutrition, there is a significant risk of suicide in AN, comparable to the level of risk in depression or conduct disorder (Latzer & Hochdorf, 2005). Purging behaviors are especially dangerous in malnourished patients, more so than in the less emaciated BN population. In general, the natural course of BN does not seem to be as severe as is the course of AN. Although some AN patients do go on to develop BN, this seems to be more the exception than the rule. EDNOS appears to be the least severe, and often remits spontaneously (Beumont & Touyz, 2003), though as there are very few treatment outcome studies of EDNOS patients at this time, is may be premature to draw conclusions such as this (Fairburn & Harrison, 2003).

The course of BN appears to be worse than is that of EDNOS, in that remission is less likely, and takes longer to occur (Fairburn & Walsh, 2002; Grilo et al., 2003). A prospective study of BN and BED patients over 5 years indicated that after marked initial improvement for both groups of patients, 50–66% of the BN patients continued to meet diagnostic criteria for at least EDNOS, if not BN, over the course of yearly assessments, but only 18% of the BED patients continued to have any sort of eating disorder after 5 years, despite the fact that few of these patients even sought treatment for their eating problems (Fairburn, Cooper, Doll, Norman, & O'Connor, 2000). Earlier longitudinal studies suggested that the progression went from less to more severe eating disorders over time, with almost half of those with subthreshold forms of AN or BN going on to develop the full disorder within 3–4 years, but it now seems that, at least for BED, there is a high remission rate and often little or no tendency for the disorder to evolve into a more serious eating disorder (Fairburn & Walsh, 2002). Unfortunately, there has still been little research on self-cure, or untreated, natural recovery or remission of eating disorders of any kind, and it remains possible that our current picture of the disorder reflects only the more serious cases that find their way into treatment (Polivy & Herman, 2002). The literature that does examine the course of the disorders suggests that the different eating disorders have different courses, with AN having the highest mortality and being least likely to remit or be cured. BN seems to be somewhat less refractory that AN, but more so than EDNOS or BED (Polivy, in press). Treated patients appear to be more likely to recover fully from an ED than patients who do not receive therapy, although this may reflect greater motivation to change on the part of those who sought treatment.

**AN is the most lethal psychological disorder**

**Table 7**
**Prognostic Indicators for Eating Disorder Outcome**

AN pretreatment factors predicting negative outcome:
- Low BMI
- Severely medically compromised
- Bulimic subtype
- Premorbid personality difficulties
- Interpersonal distrust/problems
- Previous treatment failure
- Family dysfunction
- Body image disturbance or dissatisfaction/low desired weight
- Older age at presentation

AN posttreatment factors predicting negative outcome:
- Inadequate weight gain in treatment
- General psychopathology
- Low desired weight/high drive for thinness, dieting
- Poor social adjustment

BN pretreatment factors predicting negative outcome:
- Borderline personality disorder
- Substance misuse
- Lack of readiness to change (stage of change)
- History of obesity
- High levels of bingeing and/or purging

BN posttreatment factors predicting negative outcome:
- Interpersonal/relationship problems, distrust
- Depression
- Body dissatisfaction/drive for thinness/ED cognitions
- Failure to achieve abstinence from bingeing
- Low social class/income
- Persistence of purging
- Comorbidity/general psychiatric disturbance

Based on the NICE Guidelines (www.nice.org.uk).

## 1.5    Differential Diagnosis

It has been hotly debated as to whether the various eating disorders are really different disorders, or different manifestations of a single disorder (e.g., Joiner, Vohs, & Heatherton, 2000). The core symptoms of preoccupation with body shape and weight, preoccupation with food, disturbed perceptions of one's body are present to at least some degree in all of the disorders, along with personality deficits such as feelings of ineffectiveness or low self-esteem. In fact, the "spectrum hypothesis" posits that all eating disorders are different manifestations of a single disorder or syndrome (Van der Ham, Meulman, Van Strien, & Van Engeland, 1997). Even bingeing and purging are characteristics of one major type of AN, which then leads to confusion between AN and BN[1]

---

[1]  In fact, Gleaves et al. (2000) concluded that restricting AN is more distinct from bulimic AN than bulimic AN is from BN.

(Polivy & Herman, 2002). The bulimic eating disorders appear to form a continuum of clinical severity, beginning with BED (the least severe), going on to nonpurging BN (intermediate severity), and ending with purging-type BN (the most severe) (Hay & Fairburn, 1998).

Disturbed eating can occur in other psychological disorders such as depression, but the pathological concerns about body weight and shape are not present in any other disorders, nor is overeating accompanied by compensatory purging behaviors (APA, 2000b).

## 1.6     Comorbidities

AN is associated with premordbid personality factors such as perfectionism, introversion, and low self-esteem as well as personality disorders, major depression, harm avoidance, and persistence (Karwautz, Rabe-Hesketh, Colliler, & Treasure, 2002). Both AN and BN patients frequently have comorbid anxiety disorders (particularly OCD) or depression, which may persist even after recovery from the initial eating disorder. More recent research also suggests that other anxiety disorders such as panic, generalized anxiety disorder (GAD), and post-traumatic stress disorder (PTSD) may be much more common than previously

**Comorbidities are common in eating disorders**

---

**Clinical Vignette**
**Comorbid BN and Alcohol Abuse**

Therapist: Your treatment history suggests that treating only one of your problems, either the eating disorder or the alcohol abuse, results in the second problem getting worse. It seems to be overwhelming for you to try to overcome both problems simultaneously. Does this make sense to you?

Jenny: Yeah, sort of. It's like if you take away one of my ways to deal with stuff, like, I have to use the other to get through. Like, I need to either be able to eat or to drink to get through the day.

Therapist: It sounds like you're saying that binge eating or drinking to excess are ways for you to feel better and escape your problems. Is this what you meant?

Jenny: Yeah, that's right. I really need something to dull the edge, you know? But it's getting so that it's not really working the way it used to. Now, my friends get mad if I get drunk. They say I embarrass them. And if I binge, I feel like I can't go out and be with anyone, so I'm stuck at home alone, feeling lousy. And if a guy seems interested in me, I freak out. I feel like I don't deserve his attention so I have sex with him right away. Then I feel like a slut, and hate myself, and need to eat or drink myself stupid. I can't stand this any more. I just hate myself all the time!

Therapist: Let's talk about how we might address the real problem, which isn't eating or drinking, but how you feel about yourself and treat yourself. Do you think maybe we could change what you do when you feel scared or unsure of yourself?

Patients like this exhibit multi-impulsive behavior problems. Some comorbid disorders such as this one reflect a single underlying deficit, whereas others may be more complex and involve multiple pathologies.

believed and may in fact predate the eating disorder (Swinbourne & Touyz, 2007). In addition, BN is often comorbid with substance use and panic disorders (Kaye et al., 2004), as well as impulsive behaviors such as bullying, truancy, excessive drinking, and sexual disinhibition (Kaltiala-Heino, Rissanen, Rimpela, & Rantanen, 2003). BN patients who purge also have increased comorbidity with depression, anxiety disorders, and alcohol abuse (Garfinkel, 2002).

BED has not been studied as intensively for comorbidity with other disorders, but it has been found that BED patients who report emotional abuse have a greater comorbidity with personality disorders (Grilo & Masheb, 2002).

## 1.7    Diagnostic Procedures and Documentation

**Numerous well-established standardized and semistructured diagnostic interviews and self-report questionnaires can assess the severity of ED**

There are numerous established standardized and semistructured diagnostic tests, interviews, and self-report questionnaires for ascertaining the presence and degree of severity of ED symptomatology for the various types of EDs, as well as for assessing change in these symptoms over the course of treatment. We will review the most widely used and most well-validated of these measures. The user should be aware of strengths and weaknesses of different types of diagnostic information. Standardized assessment is useful for more than just research purposes; these instruments have the advantage of providing consistent and comprehensive information regarding the presence and severity of symptoms, as well as allowing one to monitor improvements or deterioration in these (Pike, 2005). Finally, such instruments provide established norms against which to compare a given patient's clinical status.

Interviews are generally agreed to provide the most accurate information about a patient's actual symptoms, and are less influenced by self-presentation concerns that may color responses to questionnaire measures. However, extensive training, sensitivity, and expertise are required to perform a thorough and accurate interview.

---

**Table 8**
**Structured Diagnostic Interviews, Semistructured Interviews, and Self-Report Measures for Diagnosing Eating Disorders**

Structured diagnostic interviews:
- Structured Clinical Interview for Diagnosis (SCID)

Semistructured diagnostic interviews:
- Eating Disorder Examination (12th edition)
- Yale-Brown-Cornell Eating Disorder Scale
- Diagnostic Survey for Eating Disorders (DSED)

Self-report measures:
- Eating Disorders Examination (EDE-Q4)
- Eating Disorders Inventory (EDI)
- Eating Attitudes Test (EAT)
- Body Shape Questionnaire (BSQ)
- Shape and Weight-Based Self-Esteem Inventory
- Anorexia Nervosa Stages of Change Questionnaire (ANSCQ)

**Clinical Pearl**
**Measuring Physical Indices**

In assessing eating disordered patients, it is important to measure physical indices such as height and weight directly rather than relying on self-report which is generally biased and inaccurate in these patients (McCabe, McFarlane, Polivy, & Olmsted, 2001). Moreover, one must be sure that patients have not had an opportunity to load themselves with water, or put weights into their pockets before weighing these patients. However, this does not mean , that patients need to be stripped to their underwear in order to be weighed accurately. Discretion and a respectful approach are needed.

## 1.7.1 Structured Diagnostic Interviews

*Structured Clinical Interview for Diagnosis (SCID).* The general diagnostic interview used to determine what diagnosis best fits a patient's presentation, based on the DSM-IV-TR (First, Spitzer, Gibbon, & Williams, 1996; http://www.scid4.org). This interview does not, however, provide any continuous measure of severity of eating pathology, and thus should not be used in isolation, but only as part of a more extensive battery of comprehensive measures of eating disorder pathology (Pike, 2005).

The SCID is used to determine what diagnosis best fits the patients' symptoms

## 1.7.2 Semistructured Diagnostic Interviews

*Eating Disorder Examination* (12th edition). The most widely used diagnostic interview for evaluating the specific psychopathology related to eating disorders (Fairburn & Cooper, 1993). The EDE has four subscales measuring restrained eating attitudes and behaviors, eating concerns, shape concerns and weight concerns, plus individual items assessing the severity and frequency of eating disordered behavior such as binge eating or purging by various methods.

The EDE is the most widely used diagnostic interview

There have been many psychometric analyses of the EDE and its subscales, demonstrating that the subscales have good internal consistencies (ranging from 0.68 to 0.90), and the overall interview has strong discriminant validity, and modest concurrent validity, as well as demonstrated sensitivity to change over the course of treatment (Fairburn & Cooper, 1993). There is also a childhood version of the EDE available (Bryant-Waugh, Cooper, Taylor, & Lask, 1996).

*Yale-Brown-Cornell Eating Disorder Scale.* A clinical interview including a 65-item symptom checklist, as well as an additional 19 questions assessing 18 ritual behaviors and concerns, and requiring only 15 minutes to complete (Sunday, Halmi, & Einhorn, 1995).

*Diagnostic Survey for Eating Disorders (DSED).* Less widely used semistructured interview or may also be done as a self-report survey. The DSED comprises 12 sections assessing demographic characteristics, weight history, body image, dieting, binge eating, purging, exercise, behaviors related to the preceding four behaviors, sexual functioning, menstruation, medical and psychiatric history, life adjustment, and family history (Johnson, 1985).

## 1.7.3    Self-Report Measures

**The EDE-Q4 is a reasonable substitute for the EDE**

*Eating Disorders Examination (EDE-Q4).* A self-report version of the EDE interview, which assesses the frequency of bouts of overeating (both objective binge episodes in which a large quantity of food is eaten in a brief period of time accompanied by feelings of loss of control over eating, and subjective binge episodes in which the amount of food eaten is not large, but the subjective feeling of being out of control of one's eating is present). This self-report is a reasonable substitute for the EDE interview for assessing most eating disorder symptoms, except for binge eating, which tends to be overestimated by the self-report measure (Rieger, Wilfley, Stein, Marino, & Crow, 2005). The EDE-Q focuses on the past 28 days and is scored using a 7-point, forced-choice, rating scheme. Subscale scores – relating to dietary restraint, eating concerns, concerns about weight, and concerns about shape – and a global score, are derived from the 22 items addressing attitudinal aspects of ED psychopathology. Frequencies of ED (overeating and compensatory) behaviors are also assessed in terms of the number of episodes occurring during the past four weeks.

A new edition (EDE-Q6) of the EDE-Q will shortly be available. This sixth version includes minor changes to the layout, instructions, and wording of certain items based upon extensive feedback.

**The EDI is used to assess eating behavior, attitudes, and psychological traits and symptoms**

*Eating Disorders Inventory (EDI).* A standardized questionnaire measure of eating behaviors (bulimia and drive for thinness), attitudes (body dissatisfaction), and psychological traits and symptoms (e.g., perfectionism, interpersonal distrust) relevant to the understanding and treatment of eating disorders (Garner, Olmsted, & Polivy, 1983). The eight subscales of the original 64-item EDI (later versions contain additional subscales that have yet to prove their clinical utility) are assessed through questions with six forced-choice response options, only the most severe three of which contribute to the score for that subscale. The scale can be completed in approximately 15 minutes, and can be given over the course of treatment to assess improvement. A version for children is available (Garner, 1991).

*Eating Attitudes Test (EAT).* A brief, 26-item standardized test assessing eating-related symptoms (Garner, Olmsted, Bohr, & Garfinkel, 1982). Although cut-offs indicating pathology are provided, this test does not actually allow one to diagnose an eating disorder, but may be used clinically to assess amelioration of problematic eating behaviors. A children's version (the ChEat) is also available (Maloney, McGuire, & Daniels, 1988).

*Body Shape Questionnaire (BSQ).* A psychometrically sound 34-item instrument measuring concerns about body shape, feeling fat, and self-loathing due to one's weight or shape (Cooper, Taylor, Cooper, & Fairburn, 1987) that is a good indicant of AN or BN, although it does not discriminate between them especially well (Pike, 2005).

*Shape and Weight-Based Self-Esteem Inventory.* A measure of weight-related self-evaluation that involves participants selecting and rank ordering from a list of personal attributes those most important to their self-perceptions (Geller, Johnston, & Madsen 1997). Participants divide a circle into pieces reflecting how much their self-esteem is based on each of the ranked attributes. The angle of the shape and weight wedge of the circle comprises the score on this measure, which has been shown to discriminate eating disorder patients from normal young women.

*Anorexia Nervosa Stages of Change Questionnaire (ANSOCQ)*. A psychometrically validated 20-item scale for assessing aspects of anorexic symptoms and determining patients' readiness to recover from AN based on the stages of change model of self-change and recovery. It is a good predictor of self-efficacy and weight gain, especially with inpatients (Rieger et al., 2000).

The ANSOCQ determines a patient's readiness to recover

## 1.7.4    Medical Assessments

If patients are underweight, they will require a full physical state assessment by a family physician or internist. The examination should include a thorough assessment of cardiovascular state (i.e., electrocardiogram [ECG] and chest x-ray) and other special investigations as listed in Table 9. In particular, and especially if the patients are vomiting and/or purging, they should be examined for dehydration and electrolyte imbalance. A dental review is also recommended, again, particularly if the patients are vomiting. If there is amenorrhea, bone densitometry should be performed. For comprehensive medical management of eating disorder patients, both in and out of hospital refer to the Birmingham and Beumont (2004) text in the recommended reading list.

Underweight patients should undergo a full physical assessment

**Table 9**
**Medical Features and Physical Effects of Anorexia Nervosa**

| System | Medical features | Action/investigation |
|---|---|---|
| Intercellular changes | • Increased protein catabolism | Monitor pulse and blood pressure, lying and standing |
| | • Dehydration* | Monitor, care with rehydration |
| | • Edema (multiple causes) | Conservative treatment – see below |
| Endocrine | • Low serum levels of gonadotropins and steroid sex hormones, amenorrhea with an ovulation, decreased libido and low testosterone in men | No specific treatment |
| | • Altered peripheral metabolism of thyroid hormone | Check baseline thyroid function and (fasting) glucose |
| | • Raised levels of cortisol and growth hormone | Further monitoring as indicated |
| | • Hyperaldosteronism, reflex edema | Further monitoring as indicated |
| | • Hypoglycaemia | Check and monitor as indicated |
| | • Poor metabolic control in coexistent type I diabetes | Specialist management |

**Table 9** (continued)

| System | Medical features | Action/investigation |
|---|---|---|
| Electrolyte changes | • Hypokalaemia*, hypochloraemia, metabolic alkalosis | Careful K+ replacement: best orally and correct alkalosis first |
| | • Severe potassium depletion*, muscular weakness, cardiac arrhythmias, renal impairment | Monitor in all patients (may be first indication of purging) |
| | • Hypomagnesaemia (especially important in refractory cases of hypokalaemia) | Monitor in all patients |
| | • Hypocalcaemia hypo or hypernatraemia | Monitor in all patients |
| | • Hypophosphataemia* (frequently emerges during refeeding) | Monitor in all patients |
| | • Vomiting related hyperphosphataemia* | Monitor in all patients |
| Gastro-intestinal | • Acute pancreatitis | Bowel rest, nasogastric suction, and IV fluid replacement |
| | • Parotid and salivary gland hypertrophy | No specific treatment |
| | • Reduced gastric motility (and early satiety) | Smaller but more frequent meals may be preferred |
| | • Vomiting, oesophagitis, ulcerations, Mallory-Weiss tears, ruptures, chronic strictures* | Surgical referral |
| | • Gastric rupture (after bingeing) | Urgent surgical referral |
| | • Diarrhea caused by constipation and/or laxative use*, decreased peristalsis, cathartic colon, rectal prolapse, bleeding, malabsorption, protein losing gastroenteropathy | Surgical referral |
| | • Raised liver enzymes and low albumin | Monitor enzymes (aspartate transaminase and alkaline phosphatase) and albumin |
| Hematol-ogical | • Anemia# | Monitor in all patients; consider iron level and stores, B12, and folate |

**Table 9 (continued)**

| System | Medical features | Action/investigation |
|---|---|---|
| Core body temperature | • Hypothermia (may mask serious infection) | Monitor over 24 hours |
| Immune function | • Low white cell count<br>• Resistance to viral infection but susceptibility to overwhelming bacterial infection | Monitor in all patients |
| Cardiac | • Bradycardia and hypotension* | ECG in all patients, chest X-ray and Holter monitoring as necessary, conservative treatment of dependant edema |
|  | • Arrythmias[§]*<br>• Cardiomyopathy caused by ipecac use | |
| Renal | • Muscle protein catabolism, elevated creatinine, and urea | Specialist referral |
|  | • Hypokalaemic nephropathy | Specialist referral |
|  | • Low lean mass, reduced serum creatinine | No specific treatment |
|  | • Ketones, polyuria | No specific treatment |
| Skin/bone | • Osteopenia, stress fractures | Monitor bone density, consider estrogen replacement, and specialist referral |
|  | • Brittle hair/hair loss/lanugo hair | No specific treatment |
|  | • Vomiting*, dorsal hand abrasions, facial purpura, conjunctival hemorrhage | No specific treatment |
| Dental | • Erosions and perimylolysis | Dental referral |
| Reproductive | • Increased spontaneous abortion, perinatal mortality, prematurity, low birth-weight, congenital malformations | Induction of pregnancy may be effective but is injudicious; specialist supervision of pregnancy |

* Complications caused by purging behavior as well as starvation; # May be normocytic and normochronic, as characteristic of nutritional deficiency, but microcytic (iron-deficiency) is increasing as more patients become vegetarian. Copper deficiency may also play a role; [§] Cardiac arrhythmia is a common cause of death.

Reproduced with permission from Beumont et al., Royal Australian and New Zealand College of Psychiatrists Clinical Practice Guidelines Team for Anorexia Nervosa (2004). Australian and New Zealand clinical practice guidelines for the treatment of anorexia nervosa. *Australian and New Zealand Journal of Psychiatry*, 38, 663. Blackwell.

# 2

# Theories and Models of Eating Disorders

**There is no single symptom that is present in all ED patients**

We have described the three major eating disorder diagnoses, and it is clear that there are a variety of presentations, symptom patterns, and courses for eating disorders. Thus, a single cause is unlikely to account for all of these manifestations. In fact, there is no single symptom that is present in all eating disordered patients. The general symptoms of "fear of becoming fat" and "distorted perception of one's body" or "self-evaluation based exclusively on weight and shape" present in most patients imply that there is a psychological foundation for these problems, though there are possible biological features such as severe weight loss and episodes of binge eating, as well as clearly biological symptoms such as amenorrhea. A wide variety of risk factors for eating disorders have been identified (see Table 10). We will discuss some of the principal models of how these risk factors lead to the development of an eating disorder.

---

**Table 10**
**Risk Factors for the Development of Eating Disorders**

Sociocultural factors:
- Female gender (or femininity in males)
- Adolescence
- Ethnicity/western culture
- Race (Asian and Black are protective)
- Social class (poverty is protective)
- Peer and media idealization of thinness
- Urban environment

Family factors:
- Mother or father dieting, obese, or eating disordered
- Family history of affective disorders, anxiety disorders, substance use/abuse, personality disorders
- Enmeshed and/or hypercritical families

Developmental/environmental factors:
- Early childhood eating/digestive problems
- Occupations or pursuits emphasizing the body (e.g., ballet, gymnastics)
- Teasing in childhood/adolescence
- Sexual abuse or physical neglect (BN)

Genetic factors:
- Chromosome 1 (AN) or 10 (BN)
- First degree relative has an eating disorder

**Table 10 (continued)**

Physiological factors:
- Prematurity
- Birth trauma
- Birth between April and June
- Early puberty
- High BMI

Personality/psychological factors:
- Low Self-esteem
- Body dissatisfaction
- Dietary restraint / restrained eating / dieting
- Perfectionism
- Obsessiveness
- Rigidity
- Fearfulness/Anxiety
- Compromised identity
- Compliant
- Socially inhibited
- Depressed/negative affect

## 2.1    Psychological Models

### 2.1.1    Bruch's Psychological Model

Hilde Bruch formulated the first modern theory of eating disorders, describing AN as "a complex condition determined by many simultaneously interacting factors" (1975, p. 159). She was the first to point out that for these patients, eating and body shape appear to be utilized to fulfill a variety of nonnutritional needs, in particular a need for control over at least one aspect of the environment or the self, or as a means of avoiding threatening interpersonal and intrapersonal situations. Unlike many subsequent theorists, Bruch was not seduced into focusing only on patients' eating – or lack thereof – as the principal issue. She identified the primary psychological dysfunction as a severe disturbance in body image, a failure to interpret hunger and other internal signals properly, and "a paralyzing underlying sense of ineffectiveness" (Bruch, 1978, p. xxii). Like Bruch, many researchers point to the social roles and expectations for women that began to emerge in the 1960s and 1970s (and are still present today), along with pressure to attain an idealized female physique representing self-control, self-denial, and a reduced emphasis on sexuality as key contributors to the sudden proliferation of eating disorders. These eating disorders were virtually unheard of in 1970, yet within a decade, they were afflicting female adolescents at close to their present rates. Western women were breaking out of the societal cages that had constrained them, but for some, this freedom was too threatening, so, Bruch posited, they created their own psychological cages (Bruch, 1978). She described the contradictions inherent in anorexics' apparent triumphal control over their eating and bodies, when in fact their eating is controlling them.

*Patients with AN use eating to fulfill nonnutritional needs*

Bruch's ideas are still reflected in the ways in which eating disorders are assessed, treated, and understood today. The most widely used instruments for

*Bruch's ideas are still relevant today*

**Clinical Pearl**
**Malnutrition Is a Symptom, Not a Cause**

AN is essentially
a psychological
disorder

Despite the severe medical complications that follow malnutrition in AN, and the skeletal appearance, AN is essentially a psychological disorder which is reflected in the psychological etiological theories, manifestations (e.g., feelings about the self, issues around control) and treatments that have been developed to manage it. It is thus important to avoid being distracted by the malnutrition and eating behaviors at the expense of the underlying psychological issues.

assessing eating disorders reflect Bruch's observations, and many of the contributors to the disorder that she identified in the 1970s are still considered to be the major risk factors. It was Bruch who first identified what has become a major focus on sociocultural influences on eating disorders. She also pointed to dieting and the pursuit of a thin body image as precipitants of eating disorders; these are still seen as probable triggers today (Stice, 2001). The presumed contributions of perfectionism and lack of self-esteem (e.g., Polivy & Herman, 2002; Striegel-Moore, 1997) can also be traced back to Bruch's hypothesized causal underpinnings for eating disorders. Even the identity deficits that are just starting to be explored today (e.g., Wheeler, Adams, & Keating, 2001) were first noted by Bruch. As she wrote, "A common feature (in eating disordered patients) is that the future patient was not seen or acknowledged as an individual in her own right" (1978, p. 34); and "deficient in their sense of autonomy, they have difficulties in making their own judgments and opinions" (1978, p. 45). Bruch also maintained that the effects of malnutrition masked some of the underlying psychological deficits, and advocated refeeding before attempting (mainly cognitive) therapeutic intervention, as refeeding provides patients with the cognitive wherewithal to benefit from therapy. Most importantly, Bruch recognized that "The worry about being skinny or fat is just a smokescreen… The real illness has to do with the way you feel about yourself" (1978, p. 127).

## 2.1.2    Fairburn's Risk Factor Model

Fairburn recognizes the complexity of the issue and declines to offer a specific model of how eating disorders develop, maintaining that "virtually nothing is known about the individual causal processes involved, or about how they interact and vary across the development and maintenance of the disorder" (Fairburn & Harrison, 2003, p. 409). While acknowledging a genetic component, Fairburn (e.g., Fairburn & Harrison, 2003; Fairburn, Welsh, Doll, Davies, and O'Connor, 1997) hypothesize that there are two broad classes of risk factors that operate to produce eating disorders: those enhancing the general risk for psychiatric disorder (such as adverse premorbid experiences) and those that specifically increase the risk for dieting and eating problems (such as childhood or familial overweight, early menarche, and other factors that might sensitize an individual to weight or body shape). With respect to exposure to most potential risk factors, for example, BN patients resemble patients with other psychiatric disorders more than they resemble people without diagnosable psychological problems. BN patients, however, show a distinctive pattern

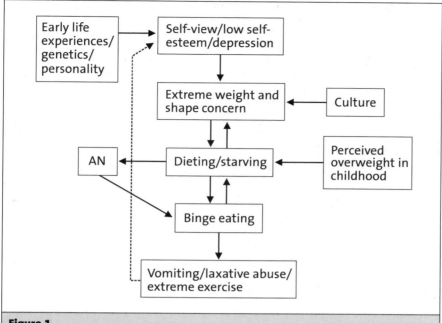

**Figure 1**
**Risk Factor Model for the Development of Eating Disorders (adapted/expanded from Fairburn's model)**

of exposure to factors likely to elevate the risk of dieting and negative self-evaluation, supporting the hypothesis that BN results from exposure to both general risk factors for psychiatric disorder and specific risk factors for dieting. In addition, Fairburn implicates personality attributes such as low self-esteem and perfectionism as contributing to the risk of developing an eating disorder (Fairburn & Harrison, 2003; see Figure 1).

## 2.1.3  The Addiction Model

The addiction model of eating disorders (Wilson, 1991, 2002) posits that there is an addictive process operating in eating disorders, particularly the bingeing disorders. Both drug abusers and binge eaters report cravings for the substance in question (drugs or food), feel out of control around these substances, use their abuse to regulate emotional states, and become preoccupied with their problem, at the same time obsessing about it and trying to keep it secret from others (Wilson, 2002). Conditioned physiological responses to food produce anticipatory secretion of insulin (Booth, 1988; Woods & Brief, 1988), which causes both craving and overeating (if only through increased tolerance to food; e.g., Booth, 1988; Wilson, 1991; Woods & Brief, 1988). Some individuals are assumed to be especially vulnerable to particular foods that produce a sort of chemical dependence (Wilson, 2002). These individuals must therefore avoid these foods, as drug abusers must give up their addictive substances.

Alternatively, self-starvation accompanied by excessive exercising may reflect an addiction to the body's endogenous opioids (Davis & Claridge,

**One controversial model hypothesizes that EDs are a form of addiction**

**Excessive exercising may lead to an addiction to the body's endogenous opioids**

1998). Both high scores by AN and BN patients on the addiction scale of the Eysenck Personality Questionnaire and correlations between addictiveness, weight preoccupation, and excessive exercising support this notion. The excessive exercising is posited to reflect a combination of addictive and obsessive-compulsive personality features that influence pathological cognitions about a need to exercise (Davis, Katzman, & Kirsh, 1999), and to serve mood regulating purposes (Davis & Woodside, 2002). Others point out that at least a subset of BN patients, specifically those who experience food cravings, exhibit a whole constellation of behaviors that could be described as "addictive" (Gendall, Sullivan, Joyce, Fear, & Bulik, 1997). These behaviors include alcohol abuse or dependence, diet pill and laxative abuse, as well as elevated levels of vomiting and excessive exercising. In fact, the neural pathways associated with the reward value of drugs and drug addiction are also involved in food palatability and craving for food, suggesting that the use of the word craving to describe the intense desire for addictive drugs and for strong desires for food may be apt (Pelchat, 2002).

**The addiction model has been criticized**

Wilson (1991, 2002) dismissed the addiction model of eating disorders for three principal reasons. First, there is little or no evidence for an "addictive personality," despite elevated rates of substance abuse in ED patients. This elevation could represent mere comorbidity (as is the case with anxiety disorders, obsessive-compulsive disorders, and depression), or the fact that those with more serious and multiple problems are more likely to seek help and receive therapeutic attention (Wilson, 1991). Second, the model does not address the core clinical characteristics of the eating disorders, most importantly, the role of dietary restraint and abnormal attitudes about the importance of body shape or the identified concomitant/underlying psychopathology of extremely low self-esteem, interpersonal distrust, and feelings of ineffectiveness (Wilson, 1991, 2002). Finally, the addiction model does not account for psychobiological connections between dieting and eating disorders. Wilson notes that bulimic behavior does not meet the criteria for an addictive disorder (i.e., tolerance, physical dependence, or craving), and the apparent similarities between binge eaters and drug addicts (such as cravings and loss of control over intake of the substance) are really superficial. For each of these similarities, there are equally salient differences. For example, in drug addicts, tolerance and conditioned dependence on the drug are ameliorated by abstinence from the abused substance; for the binge eater, however, continued restriction is counterproductive and produces more craving and binges. It is only by eating regular and predictable meals that bulimic patients can avoid the conditioned cephalic insulin responses that encourage binge eating. There is also no evidence that food is an addictive substance, and its absence does not cause withdrawal, although there are other biological consequences of starvation (Wilson, 2002). Moreover, ED (especially BN) patients do not inevitably lose control whenever they eat food the way drug addicts succumb in the presence of an addictive drug. In addition, the addictions model focuses on the single symptom of binge eating, but this is only one facet of EDs (and is not even necessarily present in all of them). Finally, binge eating seems to be to a great extent a product of dieting and restricting eating in attempts to achieve a desired slim body shape, but substance abuse does not result from initial avoidance of the substance, but the reverse. Therefore Wilson sees the addictions model as "a conceptual dead end."

**Clinical Pearl**
**BN Patients Need to Confront Their Feared Foods**

There is no scientific evidence to suggest that the abstinence model that is so effective in treatment of alcohol abuse or dependence (e.g., Alcoholics Anonymous, 12-Step Program) has any role to play in treating the binge-eating episodes in BN. BN patients need to confront their "feared" or "taboo" foods and learn to eat them in moderation, rather than trying to avoid them forever. In fact, research on food craving suggests that avoiding a particular food is likely to result in eventual over-eating of that food (Polivy, Coleman, & Herman, 2005). Avoiding foods perceived as fattening or otherwise unacceptable is actually part of the disorder in the eating disorders, so therapy involves reintegrating forbidden foods into the diet.

## 2.1.4    Cognitive Models

The cognitive behavioral theory of BN is seen by many as the primary, empirically-based theory of ED development and treatment (Fairburn, Cooper, & Shafran, 2003; Vitousek, 2002). The preoccupation with weight loss and phobic avoidance of fatness connected to an overdependence on shape and/or weight for determining self-evaluation and self-worth that characterizes these disorders is a cognitive disturbance, suggesting a strong cognitive contribution to the disorder itself (Fairburn, 2002). In addition, it has recently been proposed that in many patients, one or more of four cognitive maintaining processes interact with the core eating disorder disturbances to maintain the disorder and interfere with change (Fairburn, Cooper, & Shaffran, 2003). Specifically, these maintaining processes involve perfectionism, chronic low self-esteem, mood intolerance, and interpersonal difficulties. All of these cognitive disturbances are central to the disorders, with the behavioral manifestations (such as food restriction or dieting, and binge eating and compensatory behaviors) being secondary to the cognitive dysfunctions (Fairburn, 2002). In addition, for AN patients in particular, cognitive offshoots of the basic concerns with thinness such as dietary restraint promote a sense of moral superiority, competitiveness, and other reinforcing functions that make the disorder more difficult to dislodge (Vitousek, 2002).

There is substantial evidence that ED patients do exhibit the sorts of biases in beliefs, expectancies, and information-processing pertaining to body size and eating that have been posited to contribute to the development of eating disorders in susceptible individuals. The cognitive theory of eating disorders posits that these sorts of dysfunctional attitudes concerning physical appearance lead to other risk factors such as dietary restriction, body dissatisfaction, and overvaluing of thinness, which then contribute to the development of true EDs (e.g., Spangler, 2002). Evidence indicates that self-esteem and overconcern with weight do indeed operate as postulated, accounting for much of the variance in binge eating and purging, though in this particular study, restrained eating did not contribute further to the prediction of pathology (Byrne & McLean, 2002).

**EDs can be seen as a cognitive disturbance**

Biases in information processing resulting in or reflecting a focus on food and weight to the exclusion of other information may contribute to such psychopathological features of AN and BN as denial, resistance to treatment, and

**There is bias in information processing**

misinterpretation of therapeutic interventions. ED patients have been shown to display aberrations in information processing and memory, especially for material related to weight, shape, and food (e.g., Rieger et al., 1998). Specifically, BN patients tend to show a bias with respect to weight or shape words, whereas AN patients exhibit a bias for food words.

It is not clear, however, that this bias causes or even contributes to the disorder, as normal dieters and hungry people also show these cognitive biases (Mogg, Bradley, Hyare, & Lee, 1998). These cognitive correlates of eating disorders may thus be a result rather than a cause of food restriction and weight loss. Moreover, cognitive performance does not necessarily improve with therapy even when weight does improve in AN patients, indicating that cognitive functioning may not be not directly related to ED pathology in these patients (Green, Elliman, Wakeling, & Rogers, 1996). Further criticisms include the shortcoming that these theories fail to test adequately the longitudinal impact of cognitions in producing EDs, nor have they developed predictive ability for determining who will contract an ED and which ED will occur (Cooper, 2005). The theories do not successfully capture the full range of cognitive phenomena described by ED patients, or identify links between cognitions and behavior, affect, and physiological responses. Finally, cognitive theories seem to focus more on factors that maintain EDs than those that actually cause them.

**Maladaptive core beliefs may stem from a belief that parental care was inadequate or from sexual abuse**

On the other hand, "second generation cognitive theories" have extended the model to core beliefs about the self (Cooper, 2005). Waller and colleagues have investigated the presence of problematic core beliefs in ED patients. There is evidence of cognitive dysfunction unrelated to eating and weight in ED patients (Leung, Waller, & Thomas, 1999). Eating disorder patients were found to have elevated maladaptive cognitions related to issues such as entitlement. The role of general core beliefs was examined in a group of BN patients who were compared to normal controls. The patients differed from controls on perceived defectiveness/shame, insufficient self-control, and failure to achieve (Waller, Ohanian, Meyer, & Osman, 2000). With respect to specific symptoms of BN, emotional inhibition beliefs predicted the severity of binge eating, while defectiveness/shame beliefs predicted severity of vomiting. All of these maladaptive core beliefs appear to be related to a perception that parental care was inadequate, particularly in AN patients (Leung, Thomas, & Waller, 2000), or to childhood sexual abuse (Waller et al., 2001). Similarly, ED patients reported increases in eating-related thoughts, concerns about weight and shape, and more assumptions related to eating, weight, and shape as means to acceptance by self and others (Turner & Cooper, 2002). Moreover, they identified more negative self-beliefs in general than did nonclinical control participants, including degree of irrational and negative emotional beliefs, and associated distress, all of which was associated with negative early experiences. Waller and colleagues have developed an extended schema theory of EDs based on these data, suggesting that AN reflects primary avoidance (of negative cognitions and emotions through not eating) whereas BN represents secondary avoidance (bingeing to mask or block aversive cognitions or emotions) (reported in Cooper, 2005).

**There are second-generation cognitive theories**

Other recent modifications to cognitive theories of eating disorders have been proposed and are beginning to be tested empirically. Cooper's cognitive theory of BN describes a 'vicious circle' of automatic thoughts (of lack of control, permission to eat, and positive and negative food-related thoughts) combined with negative self-beliefs and underlying assumptions about weight, shape, eating, and the self (Cooper, 2005). There is evidence that negative mood does precede (and possibly trigger) binge eating (see, e.g., Polivy & Herman, 1993, for a review), and that feeling in control of one's eating is critical for AN patients (Cooper, 2005).

## 2.2    Predisposing Personality Theories

Certain personality traits appear to characterize many or most eating disorder patients, and are thought to contribute to susceptibility to developing an eating disorder. The Eating Disorders Inventory (EDI; Garner, Olmsted, & Polivy, 1983), an assessment instrument for measuring symptoms of eating disorders, was specifically designed to measure personality dispositions theoretically linked to eating disorders, and thought to underlie and predispose individuals to develop these disorders. Many of these were derived from Bruch's psychological theorizing. Research utilizing the EDI demonstrates that personality traits such as perfectionism, feelings of ineffectiveness (or low self-esteem), reduced interceptive awareness (or insensitivity to internal signals such as hunger and satiety), and interpersonal distrust are more likely to be found in those with eating disorders (e.g., Garner, Olmsted, Polivy, & Garfinkel, 1984; Leon, Fulkerson, Perry, & Early-Zald, 1995). Perfectionism, low self-esteem, and restrained eating have also been studied separately prospectively as personality contributors (Vohs, Bardone, Joiner, Abramson, & Heatherton, 1999; Vohs et al., 2001) in predictive models of ED development.

**Certain personality traits, such as perfectionism, characterize many patients with EDs**

Strober (1980) found evidence of obsessive personality traits, extraversion, and need for social approval prior to the development of the disorder in anorexic adolescents who had returned to normal weight. Stice's (2001) dual pathway model posits that dissatisfaction with one's body and subsequent dieting (possibly reflecting low self-esteem; Heatherton & Polivy, 1992) and a tendency toward dysphoria predict the development of eating disorders. Dieting or purging as a response to developmental and interpersonal stresses have also been implicated in the etiology of eating disorders (Nevonen & Broberg, 2000).

## 2.3    Biological/Physiological Models

### 2.3.1    Genetic Theories

The personality traits discussed above (e.g., perfectionism, obsessiveness, rigidity, fearfulness) may have genetic bases. Temperamental differences have been found in the families of patients (Grilo, 2006), supporting this view. Twin, family, and molecular genetic research have identified potential genetic contributors (e.g., Collier & Treasure, 2004; Klump & Gobrogge, 2005). Genes on different chromosomes have been identified for AN and BN, which has been interpreted as evidence that these are, in fact, different disorders (Grilo, 2006).

**There may be a genetic basis for EDs**

### 2.3.2    Hormonal Theories

**Hormonal changes and stresses may be causal factors**

Eating disorders typically develop around the time of puberty, which is a period of tremendous hormonal upheaval in young women, resulting in increased and changed distribution of body fat. The resultant curves and changes in shape do not accord with the thin physique young women idealize and pursue (see next section), leading many of them to diet. At the same time, girls are expected to pursue heterosexual interactions, placing more pressure and stress on them (e.g., Striegel-Moore, 1997). In fact, girls who experience puberty early appear to be especially susceptible to eating disorders, supporting the view that the hormonal changes and stresses associated with them may be a causal factor.

## 2.4    Sociocultural Models

**Portrayal of thin models in the media may be associated with pathological dieting behaviors**

Sociocultural models suggest that western society's idealization of thinness and constant exposure to slim "role models" in the media contribute to widespread body dissatisfaction in young women. In some susceptible individuals, this then produces pathological dieting and ultimately EDs. Some research (Mills, Polivy, Herman, & Tiggemann, 2002) suggests that exposure to idealized models may promote dieting by inspiring young women to work toward a fantasized, thinner future self. The sociobiological position suggests that the societal pursuit of thinness (and the consequent eating disorders that develop in susceptible individuals) reflect sexual competition among women (Abed, 1998). Thinness may either enhance women's reproductive prospects by making them more attractive to males or, in a contrary version, delay reproduction (by impairing fertility through emaciation) until a more propitious time. This allows young women to compete in the workplace without being burdened by having children (or, alternatively, allows them to avoid sexuality altogether, for those who find this too threatening or overwhelming). The female gender of most eating disorder patients has led to this sort of sociocultural speculation since the disorders became more widely recognized in the 1970s.

## 2.5    Integrative/Biopsychosocial Model

There are thus many models or theories about what causes eating disorders. Speculation has favored organic, familial, and psychosocial factors, which are generally hypothesized to interact in complex ways to produce the disorders (Ward, Tiller, Treasure, & Russell, 2000). This comprises the biopsychosocial model, positing an interplay between the organism, its past behavior, and its environment (biological, psychologicall, and environmental variables), which has been the principal model of eating disorder development for close to two decades (e.g., Schlundt & Johnson, 1990).

**The multiple causes of EDs are not well understood currently**

Eating disorders thus seem to have multiple causes, the interplay and integration of which are not really well understood at this time. In part, this may reflect the difficulty of gathering causal data on the development of any psychiatric disorder. Self-report, through responses to oral or written questions in interviews or questionnaires, are the main source of data in research on eating disorders; unfortunately, self-report is notoriously unreliable (Hay & Touyz 2007). Eating disorder researchers must take patients' self-descriptions at face value, if only because there are few other data available. Unfortunately, people with eating disorders are no more likely to be able to identify the source of their own disorder than the researchers who have spend the last three decades trying to do so. A full understanding of the causes of eating disorders will require much more work.

# 3

# Diagnosis and Treatment Indications

This chapter is designed to help the clinician understand how to begin to diagnose and formulate a treatment plan for patients with eating disorders. There are many different types of treatment options (which will be discussed in detail in Chapter 4) for the clinician to consider. With eating disorder symptomatology, there are potential medical complications as well as the psychological and behavioral manifestations. It should be remembered that making a clinical diagnosis of an eating disorder implies that there is a behavioral and/or psychological constellation present that is causing the patient to experience distress, disability, or possible increased risk of morbidity or even mortality (Grilo, 2006). Although there is now increasing focus on transdiagnostic treatments, specific eating disorders require their own interventions to address the disparate symptoms of the different disorders (e.g., an underweight patient with AN versus binge eating in a normal weight patient with BN). For this reason, it is necessary to determine which eating disorder diagnosis is primary in each case, and it is important to exclude other psychiatric disorders such as depression with weight loss, phobias concerning food, schizophrenia with paranoid delusions (e.g., food being poisoned) or neoplasms causing weight loss. Although the diagnostic criteria for the eating disorders have been revised repeatedly, there is little consensus concerning the specific categories into which patients with eating disorder symptoms should be placed. The fact that 30–60% of patients are given the catch-all diagnosis of EDNOS because they don't quite meet the criteria for AN or BN suggests a continuing lack of specificity in diagnosis.

**There is now an increasing emphasis on transdiagnostic treatments**

## 3.1 Diagnosing Eating Disorders

**Diagnosing AN is not always as straightforward as it may appear**

It is easy to diagnose AN in a patient who presents as severely emaciated with a clear history of dieting, fat phobia, deliberate over-exercising, and/or self-induced vomiting; however, the presenting symptoms will not always be this transparent. For example, many patients with AN go to inordinate lengths to conceal the extent of their malnutrition and failure to eat (or gain weight and grow appropriately, in a younger patient). Binge eating and self-induced vomiting in bulimic patients are usually done in secret. Because patients with bulimic symptoms feel embarrassed about their binge eating and compensatory behaviors, they feel uncomfortable disclosing the extent of the problem. Those with AN are likely to deny that there is a problem; they do not want treatment that might result in their gaining any weight.

**Clinical Pearl**
**Clues for Diagnosing Eating Disorders**

Physical/medical clues:
- BMI below the normal weight range (less than 85% of normal).
- Amenorrhea or irregular menses.
- Abdominal pains, bloating, nausea, unexplained vomiting, constipation, or sudden appearance of food allergies.
- Sore throat, excessive dental erosion or cavities, sores on knuckles (all from vomiting).
- Chest pain (constant vomiting can cause chest muscle pain).
- Requests for diet pills, laxatives, diuretics, or emetics.

Psychological/behavioral clues:
- Feeling fat and excessive concern with weight or shape.
- Depressed mood or elevated anxiety.
- Low self-esteem or feelings of ineffectiveness, lack of control.
- Insomnia.
- Social isolation, especially after former high functioning in this area.
- Perfectionism.
- Black and white/all or nothing thinking.

## 3.2     Undertaking the Initial Interviews

Eating disorder patients are reluctant to acknowledge their problems and seek treatment, and may even attempt to avoid help even when brought in by parents or friends. It should thus be remembered that the patient may not be truthful, and is often attending the interview at the insistence of others. In addition, these days it is likely that the patient (not to mention the parents) may have sought information on the internet. The patient may have encountered dramatized accounts of the disorder, or have read websites promoting the disorders, either of which may have misrepresented therapy as forced-feeding or involuntary confinement for long periods of time. The patient's fear or distrust is therefore understandable. It is thus important to engage the patient in the therapeutic enterprise (more than for other types of disorders, because of the ego-syntonic nature of eating disordered behavior). AN patients are more likely to engage in the initial interview when it is not entirely focused on their thinness and their need to gain weight.

**Patients need to be engaged in the therapeutic process**

Medical assessment including physical examination by an internist, pediatrician, or family physician is critical before psychological assessment can begin. The clinician must know the extent of medical danger from which the patient suffers, before beginning psychological treatment. Medical features of eating disorders often reflect the effects of malnutrition, which will remit with normalization of eating and weight, rather than being complications of the disorder itself. One important medical issue that clinicians must be aware of is the danger of ipecac abuse. AN and BN patients may use ipecac to induce vomiting. Repeated use of ipecac can lead to heart damage and can be fatal (Birmingham & Beumont 2004). Essential laboratory investigations are listed in the box below. These are indicated in all cases of AN and EDNOS-AN type where there is a significant weight loss and/or vomiting or purging

**Patients must undergo medical assessment before commencing psychological treatment**

**Table 11**
**Laboratory Investigations Preceding Psychological Assessment**

- Complete blood count
- Levels of serum electrolytes
- Creatinine and urea
- Blood urea and nitrogen
- Magnesium
- Phosphorus
- Aspartate aminotransferase
- Alkaline phosphatase
- Albumin
- Creatine phosphokinase
- Fasting glucose, $B_{12}$, folate, calcium
- Thyroid function test
- Urinalysis
- 12-lead electrocardiogram
- Bone mineral density test

behaviors. Patients with BN, BED, or other EDNOS will require less extensive investigation and often a complete blood count and biochemistry (electrolytes, creatinine) will suffice.

**Patients should be interviewed without parents present**

Psychological assessment should include at least one of the self-report measures listed and discussed in Section 1.7. It is important that the patient be interviewed initially on her own, without parents present (even if they insist that they need to be present for you to learn the true nature of the problem). One of the features of eating disorders is that patients feel out of control, so to engage such a person in therapy, the therapist needs to empower her to some extent. Granting her the autonomy to discuss her problem in private helps to establish rapport, and gives the clinician the opportunity to demonstrate to the patient that therapy is confidential and the parents will not be informed of what the patient says. There is one important caveat to this, which is if the patient exhibits any signs of self-harm or intention to hurt herself, she must know that this will be revealed to appropriate authorities and/or the parents. It is always best to enlist the patient's support in this process, rather than making the assessment confrontational. The clinician needs to resist the urge to focus on the patient's weight and eating, as that is what everyone else has already done unsuccessfully. Asking questions such as "How do you feel about coming here today?" or "What do you see as the major issues confronting you?" validates that not all patients feel that they have a problem, or that they may see the problem differently from what others are concerned about (Thornton, Touyz, & Birmingham, 2005). Another helpful strategy is to discuss with the patient the reasons that change is difficult and fear-provoking; this helps to show that you understand that the patient is not simply suffering from a "diet gone haywire" but that the disorder serves an adaptive purpose for her or him. In fact, one of the greatest challenges that the clinician faces in treating such patients is engaging them in "the process of change" (Cockell, Geller, & Linden, 2002) as they are generally extremely ambivalent about relinquishing behaviors which they regard as being adaptive.

**Clinicians need to resist the urge to focus on the patient's weight and eating**

In a second interview, the results of the psychological test(s) administered at the initial interview, as well as medical results should be discussed with the

**Clinical Pearl**
**Establishing Rapport**

Expecting a patient with AN to accept the clinician's judgment that she is underweight, and that treatment is necessary to regain the lost weight is naïve. The clinician is required to be innovative and explore the costs of the illness to the patient (see Appendix 8). It would not be uncommon for an underweight AN patient to be wearing several layers of clothing, so a gentle way to point out this cost to the patient (who is always cold) is that you are not cold, and ask if she is. This can help to establish rapport and demonstrate your understanding of the patient's experience, as you explain that being cold all the time is an unpleasant cost of being malnourished. This can lead to a discussion of other costs and of potential benefits from changing, as illustrated in the cost-benefit analysis of symptomatic behaviors (Appendix 8 at the end of the book).

patient. The extent of medical and psychological complications will determine the route taken in therapy. The more severely ill the patient is, the more likely it is that some form of inpatient or acute medical treatment will be needed. If there is no immediate medical or suicidal risk, then alternative psychological treatment options can be considered.

It is important that these early interviews allay the fears of both the patient and the concerned parents or friends, while at the same time providing a realistic estimate of the length and difficulty of therapy ahead. The clinician should avoid at all costs making any promises that may not be upheld.

The patient should also be encouraged to participate in a "decisional analysis" exercise so that they can become more aware of the negative consequences

| Decisional Analysis Sheet | | | | |
|---|---|---|---|---|
| | **Immediate Consequences** | | **Delayed Consequences** | |
| | **Positive** | **Negative** | **Positive** | **Negative** |
| If I remain at my current weight or continue to lose weight. | One of my few accomplishments is to lose weight. I really do well at it and it enhances my mood.<br><br>Whenever I eat I feel overcome by feelings of guilt and anxiety. I can prevent these by simply not eating. | I can't stop thinking about thoughts of food and weight.<br><br>I feel sick all time. It is awful feeling (really cold and tired and I can't sleep anymore). | I feel much more in control of my life now – also by thinking so much about my weight and shape and don't seem to be bothered by my other problems anymore. | I am becoming increasing isolated as I am avoiding my friends. There is now a real risk that I may lose them.<br><br>I always thought I wanted to have babies one day. I may put my fertility in jeopardy. |

**Figure 2**
**Sample Decisional Analysis Sheet**

of their illness rather than concentrating only on its potential benefits. An example of such a decisional analysis exercise where the patient is asked to think about the full range of immediate and delayed positive and negative consequences of AN is shown below (adapted from Touyz, Hay, & Rieger, in press).

## 3.3     Identifying the Appropriate Treatment

**There is no single agreed-upon ideal treatment for eating disorders**

There is no single agreed-upon ideal treatment for eating disorders. Several treatments have been investigated and empirically validated as useful in treating these issues. Unfortunately, no treatment is successful in even the majority of cases at this point in time.

There are different indicators that suggest different types of treatment, ranging from inpatient/medical/psychiatric treatment through to outpatient self-help.

### 3.3.1     Inpatient Hospitalization

**Hospitalization may be necessary**

Those patients with medical or psychiatric complications that are life or health threatening need to be treated in a comprehensive inpatient program that includes primary medical care, psychiatric/psychological therapy, and group, educational, and supportive therapies.

### 3.3.2     Day Hospital Treatment

**Day hospital treatment allows for regular social interaction**

As a substitute for inpatient treatment for those patients who are less medically/psychiatrically compromised but who need intensive treatment, a new development is the day hospital program. Patients usually attend for 3 to 5 days during the week, arriving early in the morning and spending the day until after dinner. Advantages include that this allows the patient to maintain some degree of schooling and social or vocational life, as well as contact with peers and family on a more regular basis. This allows for practice of the skills being learned in therapy in the patients' natural environments. Furthermore, this reduces the stigma of being hospitalized in a psychiatric unit, and is less costly than inpatient treatment while affording many of the advantages of more intensive therapy (Touyz, Thornton, Rieger, George, & Beumont, 2003).

### 3.3.3     Outpatient Treatments

**Olanzapine has shown some promise in AN treatment**

*Medication.* AN is commonly comorbid with obsessive-compulsive disorders or depression, so antidepressant medication is sometimes prescribed for AN. Selective serotonin reuptake inhibitors (SSRIs) are acceptable, but tricyclics and cisapride (for gastric motility) are generally avoided because of their possible cardiac side effects (Birmingham & Beumont 2004). Recently olanzapine, an atypical antipsychotic, has been found to improve weight gain and

**Table 12**
**Key Diagnostic Assessment Checklist**

1. Weight and height for calculating Body Mass Index (BMI: kg/m$^2$):
   If BMI is under 17.5, the likely diagnosis is AN (ICD-10; WHO, 1992).

2. Presence of binge eating and/or purging episodes:
   If yes, and frequency meets criteria (see Chapter 1), diagnosis could be AN or BN, depending on weight. If yes, but frequency is less than criteria for BN, then likely diagnosis is EDNOS. If binge eating is present but there is no compensatory behavior such as purging, starving, or exercising, then the likely diagnosis is BED.

3. Presence of severe medical complications, psychiatric risk (e.g., suicide), pregnancy, and/or severe emaciation:
   If yes, arrange specialist assessment and consider inpatient treatment.

reduce agitation and anorexic thought patterns in AN (Mondraty, Birmingham, Touyz, & Beumont, 2005). BN has been treated with SSRIs to relieve bingeing, but relapse is very common when medication is discontinued.

*Psychological Treatments.* Individual outpatient psychotherapies for eating disorders include cognitive behavior therapy, interpersonal therapy, dialectical behavior therapy, and experiential/humanistic approaches, as well as traditional psychodynamic approaches. Although manual-based therapies have been advocated for many years, particularly for BN, many patients do not respond well to these approaches, and other methods are still being investigated. These will be discussed in detail in the next chapter.

Group therapies are also used with some frequency for EDs. Assertiveness training, nutritional counseling, self-help, and guided self-change have all been advocated.

Family therapy is used most often with younger ED patients who are living at home or with married patients. This approach has proven to be particularly effective with young AN patients.

**Clinical Pearl**
**Compromising on the Amount of Weight to be Gained**

The patient will endeavor at all costs to avoid gaining weight, even while agreeing to undergo treatment. The inexperienced clinician trying to engage the resistant patient, may be tempted to agree to a compromise weight, in the hope of revising this upward as therapy progresses. This would be a big mistake. The patient will hold the therapist to whatever is promised initially and will not budge from this standpoint. Any protestation from the clinician that the initial weight gain agreed on was only provisional will simply demonstrate to the patient that the therapist cannot be trusted. If any negotiation on weight is allowed, the patient will simply attempt to negotiate an even lower target weight, and will never agree to a higher one. Thus, the weight set as a target early in treatment must be a realistic, healthy weight for the patient to attain.

## 3.4    Factors that Influence Treatment Decisions

Because there are several subtypes of eating disorders, there are many aspects to be considered when deciding on a course of treatment for any particular individual. Some common factors that have an impact on these decisions are discussed briefly below.

### 3.4.1    Age

It is generally agreed that younger patients with a shorter duration of illness have a better prognosis (Fairburn & Harrison, 2003). Age alone, however, is not a major factor in deciding what type of treatment to apply, unless the patient is deemed too young for insight therapies. A disturbing trend is the appearance of ED symptoms in younger and younger individuals. Patients as young as 8 years old are now being diagnosed with EDs, and clearly are not capable of insight-oriented psychotherapy.

### 3.4.2    Gender

As far as we know, men and women respond equally well to psychological therapies for EDs (Braun, Sunday, Huang, & Halmi, 1999), but there is still insufficient data to draw any firm conclusions (Carlat & Carmago 1991). Some patients do appear to feel more comfortable with a therapist of the same sex; this is particularly true for young women who have been sexually abused.

### 3.4.3    Race/Ethnicity

EDs are primarily thought of as disorders of the White middle and upper classes, but are now appearing more regularly in minority populations, particularly in populations that are undergoing or have undergone Westernization (e.g., Japan; Nakai, 2003), or in minority members who have moved to a Western environment (Soh, Touyz, & Surgenor, 2006). However, there are many controversies about how to interpret findings from cross-cultural studies from what is meant by "Westernization" to the nature of eating disorder symptoms and doubts about the validity of the application of the APA diagnostic criteria across different cultures (Hoek, van Hoeken, & Katzman, 2003). In addition, there has been a paucity of research in to patterns of health care use and treatment needs across different cultural and ethnic groups. (See Section 4.7 below for more discussion of these issues in treatment.)

### 3.4.4    Patient Preference for a Particular Type of Therapy

**Patient preference should be considered**

Most patients resist the idea of hospitalization for ED therapy. As long as they are not medically compromised, it is usually prudent to agree to at least a trial of outpatient treatment, with a clear understanding that if this is unsuccessful, inpatient treatment will be undertaken. Patients are usually agreeable to this. Younger patients may be resistant to a family-based approach, opting for individual treatment instead. If, however, the therapist decides that the problem is family-based, then it may be necessary to get the family involved, at least for a few sessions. For BN, the direct approach of cognitive behavior therapy (CBT) has been shown to be no more effective in the longer term than a more indirect interpersonal psychotherapy (IPT), so both approaches should be discussed with the patient.

### 3.4.5 Clinical Presentation

For patients who present with severe emaciation or other medical complications or suicide risk, inpatient treatment is almost a necessity (Hay & Touyz, 2007). Outpatient support groups may be sufficient for subthreshold patients, or mild cases of EDNOS or BED (e.g., an AN patient with a BMI of 17 who is not suicidal and/or severely medically compromised). It should be remembered that hospitalization is the treatment of last resort for the most recalcitrant or severely disturbed patients, and the majority of patients will be treated in outpatient therapies or community settings. Some treatment organizations also offer group therapy for patients and their families. Outpatient treatment has the distinct advantage of allowing for more generalizability of treatment gains to the patient's natural environment because the patient remains in their natural environment during the course of therapy.

**Hospitalization should be the treatment of last resort**

### 3.4.6 Comorbidity

Comorbid presentations of EDs with other disorders such as depression, anxiety disorders, obsessive compulsive disorder (OCD), substance abuse, or personality disorders may call for combined treatment approaches (e.g., use of both medication and psychotherapy). Both disorders must be addressed; however, this may prove difficult for inexperienced therapists. For example, one of the common dilemmas faced by clinicians in the treatment of AN is the presence of marked OCD symptoms such as elaborate rituals which interfere with the treatment of the eating disorder. Few OCD treatment facilities will accept severely malnourished AN patients, and will insist that they be refed before referral for treatment of their OCD symptoms. There is thus little option except to treat both of the disorders concurrently.

**Comorbidities may call for combined treatment approaches**

**Clinical Pearl**
**Understanding the Compulsive Rituals in AN**

AN patients usually fear contamination by calories rather than by germs. As a result, it is being argued that the obsessive compulsive disorder (OCD) symptoms found in AN patients are most likely to be the result of malnutrition/starvation (see Keys study, Section 4.1.1) and/or an exaggeration of a preexisting obsessive compulsive personality disorder (OCPD), rather than a true OCD.

On the other hand, not all therapists with the experience and expertise to treat EDs also have skill in treating substance abuse or other comorbid conditions. It is not clear whether it is preferable to have two skilled therapists jointly treat the comorbid patient, or whether one therapist should attempt to address both disorders (Coelho, Thornton, Touyz, Lacey, & Corfe, 2007).

### 3.4.7    Treatment History

Many patients report that they have been treated unsuccessfully with evidence-based treatments such as CBT. There is now considerable clinical evidence to show that such patients may have been told that they are receiving CBT when this is not necessarily the case. A careful inquiry as to the components and nature of the previous treatment will help to clarify whether the appropriate treatment was actually administered. In circumstances in which the original therapy was not faithful to the treatment orientation, another trial is warranted. However, when patients have already been unsuccessful with a particular approach, it may be more beneficial to utilize one of the alternative therapies available.

With regard to inpatient treatment, many units adopt similar treatment regimens. Often there is little to be gained by moving from one unit to another, unless there is a justifiable reason for such a move (e.g., personality conflict between therapist and patient). It is not uncommon for EDs to have a relapsing course, so multiple admissions to hospital are not necessarily a poor prognostic indicator, but may simply reflect the natural course of the disorder. It is also important for patients to understand the difference between a lapse and true relapse. It often takes many years for a patient with AN to fully recover even in the hands of a skilled therapist. This is a good example where peer support can be extremely helpful in maintaining the motivation of the therapist.

Some patients with BN also have an underlying personality disorder, such as borderline personality disorder. These patients often require repeated treatment regimens, as they follow a fluctuating course punctuated by frequent crises that detract from the goals of therapy.

Finally, patients with AN often successfully manipulate a discharge from therapy prior to reaching an acceptable goal weight. The promise is that they

**Clinical Pearl**
**A Lapse Versus a True Relapse**

Not unlike a pilot in command of a commercial jet liner who is likely to encounter turbulence during a flight, the ED patient faces the distinct possibility of having to confront the vicissitudes of daily life. Notwithstanding the fact that the pilot is highly trained and skilled to deal with turbulence, it cannot always be avoided. When it does occur, the plane shakes violently often causing significant distress to the passengers but in nearly all cases, the pilot uses well rehearsed maneuvers to restore calm. So it is with ED patients. Despite the fact that patients have been well trained in preparing for a lapse when faced with a real life dilemma, they may resort once again to either bingeing or vomiting, or, in the case of AN patient, begin to lose some weight. However, these symptoms are often much less severe (i.e., smaller binges which occur less frequently or only a few pounds lost [lapse] than was the case initially which would constitute a true relapse).

will gain more weight on their own, but this rarely materializes. Such patients gradually lose weight until they need to be hospitalized and treated once again. Therapists should not be disillusioned by such lapses, but should anticipate that this might occur and deal with it accordingly.

# 4

# Treatment

## 4.1 Methods of Treatment

Psychological
treatments are
regarded as the
primary treatment
for EDs

Psychological therapies are now regarded as "first-line" in the treatment of eating disorders. This section will focus on the two "best evidence" therapies for EDs, namely cognitive behavior therapy for BN (CBT-BN) and family therapy for AN. While it is not known which, if any, treatment approaches are most commonly used world-wide in AN, there is a large literature describing the use of CBT in the treatment of AN. Several variants of CBT have been developed for BED, often in conjunction with behavioral weight control/loss regimes. Research has been limited for specific EDNOS groups, but their management mirrors that of the more definitive eating disorder they most resemble.

Most treatment for BN and EDNOS is conducted on an outpatient basis and offered as individual therapy, or sometimes adaptations of individual therapy to a group approach. While evidence is thus far insufficient to support outpatient over in-patient programs (Meads, Gold, Burls, & Jobanputia, 1999), the focus of treatment of AN has also moved from long-term in-patient programs with outpatient follow-up, to outpatient care with hospital backup (Garner & Needleman, 1997). Care is usually offered in individual or group sessions, and family therapy is usual in child or adolescent settings. However, it is thought that severely ill patients are best treated in a specialized unit, at least until nutritional state is restored (Touyz, Garner, & Beumont, 1995). Inpatient regimes have moved away from strict programs emphasizing weight gain towards more "humane" approaches that place less emphasis on weight gain and more on psychological, family, and interpersonal issues, and shorter inpatient treatments followed by partial or day hospitalisation or outpatient programs (e.g., Touyz & Beumont, 1997; Touyz, Beumont, Glaun, Phillips, & Cowie, 1984). These approaches are popular in that they can incorporate individual, group, and family therapies, as well as refeeding, plus they are cost-efficient and allow patients to continue with education and maintain contact with family and friends. The frequency and duration of therapy is diverse and there is no commonly accepted "standard."

### 4.1.1 Psychoeducation

Psychoeducation
is an integral
component in
treatment

Psychoeducation is integral to all psychological approaches in eating disorders and is a key feature in the initial stages of CBT (see below, Section 4.1.2). The aim is to give patients and their families an understanding of the disorder so that they are better informed about the problems and their treatments. Many self-help books devote almost half their text to such information (see Table

**Table 13**
**Sources of Psychoeducation Information**

- Fairburn, G. C. (1995). *Overcoming binge eating.* New York: Guilford.
- Cooper, P. (1995). *Bulimia nervosa and binge eating. A guide to recovery* (reprint ed.). London: Robinson Press, and New York: New York University Press.
- Schmidt, U., & Treasure, J. (1993). *Getting better bit(e) by bit(e): A survival kit for sufferers of bulimia nervosa and binge eating disorders.* New York: Psychology Press.
- Treasure, J. (1997). *Anorexia nervosa: A survival guide for families, friends, and sufferers.* New York: Psychology Press.
- Website for the Academy of Eating Disorders: www.aedweb.org.
- Website for the Center of Excellence for Eating Disorders: www.rch.org.au/ceed.

13). Consumer group web-sites are another good resource for patients. At the least, practitioners should have a prepared list of books, websites and other handouts (see appendices) to provide at the time of the initial interview.

It is important to educate the patient not only about the disorder, but about the severity of the problem for each individual. Patients often deny that they are really ill, or incapacitated by the eating disorder, especially in AN. For these patients this can be particularly problematic in that it interferes with their motivation to change. A helpful tool for encouraging patients to reflect on their current state is the "RU (where aRe yoU now) curve." To use this tool, the therapist has his or her patients indicate on the curve in red ink what they believe their status to be on each of five dimensions of current risk. Then the therapist indicates his or her opinion of the patient's status using blue ink so that patients can see the discrepancy between their judgments and those of the clinician. This can be used as a dynamic tool throughout therapy to monitor progress and give feedback in areas where patients still hold a distorted view of their status. For each of the five dimensions, (medical status = M; nutritional status = N; social functioning = S; emotional distress = E; weight status = W), a letter is placed on the curve to indicate patients' and therapists' views about each dimension at each time, allowing for a direct comparison (see Figure 3).

**The RU Curve can be a helpful tool in assisting patients to develop a more realistic appraisal of their illness**

Psychoeducation also includes improving patients' understanding of the psychological effects of restrictive dieting and how many distressing symptoms they are experiencing, including mood disturbance and binge eating, result from effects of starvation. While it is old, the Keys study is still very relevant, and it has been supported by subsequent research, with numerous empirical controlled studies documenting that people who restrict eat more when provided with a standardized meal than normal controls in an unrestricted eating group. This information is also very helpful for families and carers, and lessens the tendency to "blame" patients for their symptoms. Sufferers are often very relieved to know that their problem is not rare, they are not alone, and that some of their feelings, thoughts, and behaviors are direct consequences of the eating disorder. This is especially so for AN where patients and families are often intrigued by the results of the Keys starvation study (see Vignette below), and for bulimic patients who are relieved to hear that others do the same bingeing and purging behaviors that they do.

**Your RU Curve – Where aRe yoU now?**

**Instructions:**
Use a separate curve for each of the following categories
(a) medical status (M)
(b) nutritional status (N)
(c) social functioning (S)
(d) emotional distress (E)
(e) weight status (W)

**RU Category**

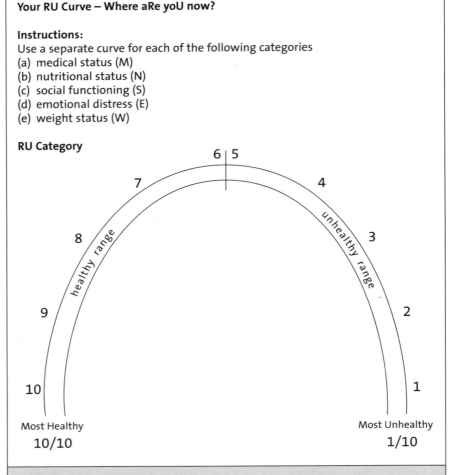

**Figure 3**
**Sample RU Curve**

*Note:* Clinicians can be as creative as they like with the RU curve and develop their own categories to best suit the patient's current situation (e.g., ruminations about food, sleep, alcohol intake, etc.).

**Clinical Vignette**

**The Keys Study/The Minnesota Starvation Study**

It is often helpful to educate patients about the classic study of human starvation done by Ancil Keys and his colleagues during World War II and published in 1950 (Keys, Brozek, Henschel, Mickelsen, & Taylor, 1950).

Thirty-six young men who were conscientious objectors to the war volunteered to participate in a study in which for six months they ate only half of their normal food intake in an attempt to lose 25% of their body weight. In fact, their food intake had to be reduced further because they could not keep losing to the required level (the mean amount ultimately lost was only about 24%). They suffered many of the symptoms now associated with an eating disorder, such as obsessive thoughts about food, studying recipes, deciding to become chefs, dreaming about food, loss

**Clinical Vignette**
**(Continued)**

of interest in sexual activity (photographs of pin-up girls were replaced by recipes), prolonging eating, cutting their food into little pieces, increasing the use of salt and spices, rigidity about food preparation, gum chewing, drinking large amounts of coffee and tea, and, during refeeding, binge eating followed by vomiting. Other psychological effects included severe depression and mood swings, irritability and outbursts of anger, compulsive behaviors and self-harm (one cut off three fingers). In addition, the men became isolative and withdrawn, with food and eating taking precedence over interest in sexual and other relationships or other activities.

## 4.1.2 Cognitive Behavior Therapy (CBT) for BN

A specific form of CBT has been developed for BN termed CBT-BN (Fairburn, Marcus, & Wilson, 1993; National Institute for Clinical Excellence, 2004). While it was developed for BN, it has many elements that are very helpful and easily adapted to treatment for AN, BED, and EDNOS. CBT is most commonly provided as an individual therapy although it has been found to be as effective in group format in BN (Chen et al., 2002) and in other disorders such as EDNOS (Nevonen & Broberg, 2006).

*The "nuts and bolts" of conducting CBT for BN*

CBT-BN uses three overlapping phases (in adults) for a time limited to 19 sessions over 20 weeks. CBT-BN is a manualized therapy, and many therapists may choose to follow a published form such as found in Fairburn's self-help book (*Overcoming Binge Eating*, 1995). Manuals are particularly helpful in the "guided self-help" situation where the therapist is not a specialist and where use of guided self-help manuals has been found to be efficacious (Banasiak, Paxton, & Hay, 2007; Sobell & Sobell, 1998).

*Phase one* of CBT-BN aims to educate the patient about BN. The cognitive-behavioral model that there is a self-perpetuating cycle of weight concerns, binge eating, and compensatory behaviors is presented and personalized for the sufferer. Together with the patient, the therapist points out the cycle and how it works, with details pertinent for the particular patient. These might include a history of abuse in childhood, exposure to a "weight-loss" culture through ballet dancing or having lost weight through an illness such as glan-

---

**Clinical Pearl**
**Instituting a Meal Plan**

- Decide on times for eating (plan ahead when you'll eat).
- Decide ahead of time what food to have (don't wait until you're starving).
- Stick to the plan.
- Avoid "making up" for binges or special meals (no single eating episode will ruin your plan – just keep going, no starving or meal skipping allowed!).
- Resist urges to binge and/or vomit – use distractions and alternate activities (make a list of these to refer to as needed).
- Include all foods, even if in very small quantities (no forbidden foods! – remember, a calorie of lettuce is the same to your body as a calorie of chocolate).
- Enjoy your food – eating is supposed to be pleasurable.

dular fever and experiencing the positive effects of this from complimentary comments by others. In this phase patients are helped to increase the regularity of eating, and to resist the urge to binge or purge. Nutritional counseling is provided concerning "normal" eating patterns and dietary needs and emphasizing the importance of eating regular meals, not going for long periods without eating, and exploring strategies that help to reduce binge eating and purging such as planning ahead what the person might do after eating. (Beumont, Beumont, Touyz, & Williams 1997). It can be helpful to direct patients to websites for supplementary information (as listed in Table 13).

In addition, patients are guided in commencing symptom diary records (see Appendix 6) and a food diary (see Appendix 7). They should do this regularly, at least once per day, if not more often, and as close as possible to the eating or other events recorded. It is best to have a separate sheet of paper or diary page for each day. For those patients who have electronic diaries, these records are easily incorporated into their organizers, allowing them to do these records in an electronic format which may be more appealing to younger patients. This also allows for immediate recording as the events are experienced. It is essential to bring these records to each therapy session.

**Food records can be incorporating into electronic diaries**

**Clinical Pearl**
**Why Food Diaries Are So Important**

It is often difficult for patients to overcome their understandable reluctance to write down the details of their binge eating and extreme weight control behaviors in the food diary. It helps to explain that the treatment has been studied with and without the keeping of such diaries, and has been found to be more effective with this element. Also, "just" keeping the record in itself (i.e., self-monitoring) has been found to bring about improvements (Fairburn, 1995).

**Broader food choices can be illustrated by means of the food pyramid**

*Phase two* introduces procedures to reduce dietary restraint. It is important to promote broader food choices and to revisit the "food pyramid" (see Appendix 10; for further information consult www.mypyramid.gov/guidelines). Reassure patients that they are not expected to eat all the food at one sitting, but to spread their consumption over the course of a day. Patients make lists of foods that cause them the most anxiety (in order of least to most) – these often being "forbidden foods" only consumed in binges. They then introduce to their diet the least- to the most-feared foods in order. This is in a gradual process – one or two foods being introduced each week. At this phase, cognitive

**Clinical Pearl**
**The Supermodel Story**

The following hypothetical story can be discussed:

It is estimated that hundreds of thousands of girls dream of becoming a supermodel, but only a few will actually complete a modeling course. Only a few of these will eventually apply for modeling jobs, and only a few of these will actually find a job. Of those who get a job, only a few will be considered as good enough to become supermodels. Out of all these girls, perhaps one (maybe!) will become a supermodel!

procedures supplemented by behavioral experiments are used to identify and correct dysfunctional attitudes and beliefs and avoidance behaviors. Patients are encouraged to reflect on their weight, normal weight ranges, and to gently challenge cognitive distortions (see Appendix 9) and inappropriate cultural expectations of "ideal" weights that are unachievable for over 90% of people.

Problem solving is also introduced at this phase. This incorporates five steps:

1. Define the problem.
2. Generate solutions.
3. List advantages and disadvantages of each solution.
4. Choose a solution.
5. Try it out and review your success; if unsuccessful, revisit other potential solutions.

---

**Clinical Pearl**
**Problem Solving**

---

Problem solving rests on the premise that there is no problem that cannot be solved. If a patient is "stuck" in therapy, problem solving can be used to help move forward. For example, a problem may be that the patient can never eat lunch. The therapist and patient explore this. The problem is more closely defined as the patient dislikes eating around others, and there is little privacy at her workplace. In order to help the patient generate solutions, the therapist proposes two extremes: (a) no change, or (b) resigning the job. Both have advantages and disadvantages. This prompts the patient into generating other solutions that may have some more advantages, e.g., going for a walk outside at lunch time and eating outdoors. One strategy is to teach patients the serenity credo: *Grant me the serenity to accept the things I cannot change; the courage to change the things I can; and the wisdom to know the difference.*

---

*Phase three* is the maintenance phase. Relapse-prevention strategies are used to prepare for possible future set-backs. Arrangements may be made for one or two follow-up sessions in the months after therapy ends. It is important to address relapse-prevention strategies and discuss what to do about lapses starting from at least the final quarter of sessions. It is also useful to reflect with patients on their improvements, look back over diary records and repeat the rating scales used at the start of therapy. For example, many clinicians use the EDE-Q (Fairburn & Cooper, 1993; see Section 1.7.3).

**Relapse-prevention strategies need to be discussed**

---

**Clinical Pearl**
**Dealing with Lapses**

---

- Lapses will occur.
  - Both therapist and patient should be prepared.
  - It's *never* back to "baseline" – there is some improvement retained.
  - Refer back to monitoring sheets and records that show improvement (e.g., vomiting was daily initially and is now only twice a month).

- Compile a record of strategies to cope with lapses.
  - Resume monitoring.
  - Review distraction techniques or other methods used earlier.
  - Learn from the lapse – what went wrong and why.

---

**Clinical Vignette**
**Relapse in a BN Patient**

Patient:     I've had a terrible week. Treatment isn't working; I'm bingeing and vomiting again.
Therapist:   I'm sorry to hear that. How many times did you binge this week?
Patient:     I binged and vomited twice on Wednesday.
Therapist:   Tell me about that. What were you doing before you started bingeing?
Patient:     I went to visit my mother, and we had a fight. I was so upset I didn't eat lunch or anything all afternoon. I came home early from work, and felt bingey, so I just started to eat.
Therapist:   Remember when you were monitoring your eating, and we discussed the importance of regular meals? Do you think that skipping lunch might have contributed to your problem eating later?
[The antecedents to the binge are discussed in more detail before the therapist moves on.]
Therapist:   So we see that when you're upset for some reason and you skip a meal, this leads to problems later on with regulating your eating, and you wind up bingeing. But remember, if we look back at your monitoring sheets, when you first came, this was happening every day, not just once in a while. You have made great progress in dealing with this. This is merely a lapse, which often occurs for people learning to overcome bulimia nervosa. You have not relapsed; we can learn from this lapse and prevent it next time. It's like learning to ride a bicycle. When you start, you ride for a bit and then fall off, but you get up and you ride for longer before you fall again.

## 4.1.3    Cognitive Behavior Therapy for AN

**Treatment of AN has changed over the years**

There has been a dearth of empirical research on the treatment of AN; much of what has been written to date has been driven by philosophy and clinical experience (Pike, Carter, & Olmsted, 2005). In some ways, we have reached a position which is diametrically opposed to what it was previously. Sir William Gull, who coined the term AN in 1874, advocated the removal of the patient from her family whereas the current Maudsley approach requires the parents to play an integral role in the treatment of their offspring. Furthermore, the early enthusiasm that greeted the arrival of behavior modification programs in the 1970s began to wane by the year 2000 when more lenient programs replaced the strict operant conditioning regimens.

The introduction of such lenient behavioral programs were accompanied by a greater focus upon psychological interventions rather than merely weight gain.

---

**Clinical Pearl**
**Treating Both the "Anorexia" and the "Nervosa" in AN**

The primary focus on weight gain may be effective in treating the "anorexia" but fails to adequately address the psychological aspects of the disorder, "the nervosa" (Pike, Carter, & Olmsted, 2005, p. 10).

When psychological treatments fail to deliver the desired treatment outcome, one can usually turn to pharmacological interventions. Sadly, this has not materialized in the treatment of AN although there is now some emerging evidence that olanzapine, which was developed for the treatment of schizophrenia, is showing some promise with relieving the obsessional ruminations that cause so much distress to those suffering from AN (Mondraty et al., 2005). In case you were starting to worry about what you were going to tell your next adult patient with AN, treatment options are available. Over the past few decades, much has been written on the treatment of AN; however, most of the proposed treatments have not been empirically investigated.

**Olanzapine may relieve obsessional contemplation**

There is now a smorgasbord of options for the adult patient with AN, including well-established outpatient treatments, innovative day hospital programs, and inpatient hospitalization if necessary. Such programs use a combination of techniques including nutritional counseling (often by experienced nutritionists working exclusively in the field of eating disorders), behavioral interventions, cognitive techniques, exercise counseling, as well as family interventions. The development of more effective outpatient based treatments, including day hospitals, is especially welcome in the United States where it is now becoming increasingly difficult to access inpatient beds (the average 149.5 day stay in 1984 was reduced to 23.7 days in 1998; Pike et al., 2005). In the outpatient setting, the duration of treatment is generally 1–2 years. This is considerably longer than treatment for other disorders such as anxiety disorders, but as Garner, Vitousek, and Pike (1997) explain, "The longer duration of treatment is required in most cases… because of the time required to overcome motivational obstacles, achieve appropriate weight gain, and occasionally implement inpatient or partial hospitalization" (p. 97). The patient is usually seen twice weekly for the first month, then weekly for the next eleven months, and then every other week to once per month for a further 6 months.

## The Development of CBT Interventions in AN

It will probably come as no surprise that the current CBT framework for AN is actually based upon the pioneering work of Aaron Beck and his colleagues (Beck, 1976; Beck, Rush, Shaw, & Emery, 1979) who were responsible for the development of CBT for depression. Clinicians who already have expertise in the delivery of CBT will find the principles involved to be similar, but with one major difference: Most patients with AN view their symptoms as ego-syntonic and are often petrified by the thought of change. Working with such patients poses unique challenges that ultimately make treatment both an interesting and rewarding exercise.

## CBT – Establishing the Therapeutic Relationship

As with any other psychological intervention, the establishment of a solid therapeutic relationship is a *sine qua non* for successful outcome. This is especially so in an AN patient who is usually frightened and/or bewildered by both her symptoms and her fear of treatment, i.e., that it will make her fat.

Those nonspecific therapist qualities of warmth, empathy, respect, openness, compassion, honesty, and flexibility are absolutely essential in the treatment of patients with AN. Some of the important factors to consider when

**Nonspecific therapist qualities**

---

**Clinical Vignette**
**Fear of Losing Control**

Patient: I can't possibly follow the meal plan prescribed by the dietitian. She has included foods full of fat, and if I eat then I will gain weight and get fat. Every advertisement you now see says you should eat less fat to avoid becoming obese. If I eat what she wants me to eat then I may get used to all those fattening foods and get to like them. Then what will happen? I will lose control and hate myself and want to die.

Therapist: Do you believe that you are in control of your food intake now?

Patient: Obviously, what do you think – I avoid all high calorie foods and never lose control by eating those disgusting junk foods like doughnuts, chips, or chocolates. I know I can't get fat by sticking to only fruit and vegetables.

Therapist: Most modern homes these days have climate control. Do you know what this is?

Patient: Yes, we have it at home. You can control the temperature inside the house. When it's cold, you make it warmer and when it's hot, you cool the house down.

Therapist: You said you were in control of your weight. That means like the climate control in your home, you can allow your weight to go up or down.

Patient: No, not up, only down.

Therapist: That doesn't seem right. You don't seem to have control over your weight as you can only move it in one direction.

Patient: I haven't really looked at it that way before. I can only move it one direction not the other – maybe I am not really in control of my weight.

Therapist: What you experience is not unusual. Most patients fear that they will lose what they consider to be control when they start eating again. We know from research that when you begin to regain weight, you can experience episodes of intense hunger or cravings for food. These usually disappear quickly when you have reached your weight range and maintained it for a while. We are aware of this phenomenon and will help you through it.

Patient: I'm pleased that you understand what I am going through.

---

establishing a therapeutic alliance with an AN patient are documented below (adapted from Pike et al., 2005).

- You need to refrain from imposing your will on the patient – this has usually been tried previously and failed.
- You need to develop "accurate empathy" in that you view the world from the patient's stand-point and understand what she feels.
- You need to feel confident in taking an active role in treatment and, especially in the early sessions, providing a clear direction.
- You need to introduce the structure and goals for treatment.
- You need to emphasize the point that successful CBT treatment requires a collaborative approach (i.e., you and your patient work together to ensure that the goals of each session are accomplished to your mutual satisfaction).
- You will have succeeded in your endeavors when the patient becomes "her own therapist." This is especially important because the patient will need to continue to implement the strategies she has acquired long after the formal treatment sessions have come to an end.

- The transfer of strategies and skills to the patient enhances her sense of self-efficacy thus contributing to recovery from AN.
- You need to be realistic as to what can be achieved in both the short (first few weeks to months) and long (months to sometimes years) term. Otherwise both you and your patient will tend to downplay small but significant changes in attitude and behavior leading to feelings of impotency and possible treatment failure.

In summary, the essential framework for CBT in AN is the normalization of eating behavior to ensure consistent weight gain to a target range by drawing attention to the interaction between prevailing cognitions, feelings, and behaviors that are connected to the AN. The main principle of CBT that characterize treatment have been summarized by Garner, Vitousek, and Pike (1997, p. 109).

1. The acceptance of conscious experience rather than unconscious phenomena.
2. Focus upon belief, assumptions, schematic processing, and meaning systems as mediating variables for maladaptive behaviors and emotions.
3. The employment of questioning as a prominent therapeutic strategy.
4. Active participation by the therapist in treatment.
5. The essential contribution of homework sessions which need to be integrated into each treatment session. If you don't stress the importance of it and pay particular attention to it, then the patient will be less likely to comply.

A practical and often helpful strategy for the patient is the development of a collaborative diagnostic formulation on a white board or paper. Here all past and present factors that are contributing to and/or maintaining the disorder can be diagrammatically presented. Both the patient and therapist should retain a copy and it should be placed on the table in the therapy room at each session. Such a formulation constitutes a work in progress and should be updated as additional information becomes available. It has been our experience that this allows the patient to make sense of her current predicament and reduces the potential for denying both the costs and burden of the illness.

**Collaborative diagnostic formulation can be extremely helpful**

Finally the importance of self-monitoring cannot be underestimated and is one of the important components of CBT. Patients should be strongly encouraged not only to monitor their food/drink intake, but also the context in which this occurs (see the self-monitoring form provided in Appendix 7).

**Patients need to monitor intake of food and drink**

Placing social and emotional experiences in the context of the eating disorder assists the patient in identifying how these experiences affect their

---

**Clinical Pearl**
**Keeping Track of Intake**

Patients should pay attention to the following questions:

1. What did you eat or drink?
2. How much did you eat or drink? (Please quantify – i.e., one slice of buttered toast with cheese and tomato)
3. Where were you when you ate and/or drank?
4. Were you alone or with others?
5. What were your thoughts at this time?
6. What emotions were you experiencing?

daily lives. While the patient can complete her own self-monitoring tasks, it is best that the therapist weigh the patient (on the same scale each time) at the commencement of the session, preferably not more than once per week in outpatient treatment (Touyz, Lennerts, Freeman, & Beumont, 1990). The patient should be discouraged from weighing herself at other times as this is likely to result in her becoming upset and reinstituting food restriction (if weight gain has been achieved).

## Motivation for Treatment

As so many patients are poorly motivated, motivational assessment and enhancement is particularly important as it allows the therapist to individualize treatment depending upon the capacity of the patient to be able to respond to it. The role of motivational enhancement therapy (MET) in treatment patients with AN has been described in detail in Section 4.2.6.

---

**Clinical Pearl**
**Survival as a Therapist in AN**

Those clinicians working exclusively in the field of eating disorders, and more specifically with AN patients, are often asked the following question: "How can you survive dealing with such demanding and poorly motivated patients – how do you stay sane?" The answer is two-fold. (a) First, we are realistic in terms of our expectations and goals – treatment can be a frustrating and somewhat turbulent journey no matter how skilled you are as a therapist. To survive, requires endurance and the patience of Job. It can takes years! (b) Second, when possible, we establish a network of colleagues such as dietitians and physicians as well as colleagues in treatment centers to whom we can turn to when the situation demands it, e.g., when there is an urgent need for hospital admission.

---

## Core Components of Treatment: Confronting the "Anorexia Wish"

Patients with AN often beg to work psychologically to resolve underlying emotional conflicts which would then allow them to commence eating again and to regain weight. They insist on wanting to put weight gain on hold until they have dealt with the "real" issues.

---

**Clinical Pearl**
**"Compliance" Without Actual Weight Changes**

In AN, it is imperative that the therapist not fall into the trap of being seduced by patients' apparent psychological insights and then disregarding the fact that they are not gaining significant amounts of weight, or are, worse yet, continuing to lose weight. Whether the clinician likes it or not, this weight issue will ultimately have to be addressed. This is best achieved in a nonconfrontational manner.

---

However tempting this request may be, it simply doesn't work in the longer term. One cannot recover from AN unless one gains weight. What is required here is the "two track" approach described by Garner et al. (1997), see Table 14 below.

**Table 14**
**The Two-Track Approach in Treating Patients with AN**

| Food and Weight Themes | Psychological Themes |
|---|---|
| 1. Weight | 1. Poor self esteem |
| 2. Bingeing | 2. Poor self concept |
| 3. Vomiting | 3. "Bad" perfectionism |
| 4. Dieting | 4. Emotional regulation |
| 5. Over exercising | 5. Impulse control |
| 6. Laxative abuse | 6. Family dynamics |
| 7. Medical complications | 7. Interpersonal functioning |

The therapist must ensure that the patient ultimately addresses both themes, but at the outset it is best to begin with the food and weight themes. The Keys study (see Section 4.1.1) is of value here as it can be scientifically argued that many of the symptoms of AN are the result of malnutrition, and that there is a significant interplay between the two approaches to treatment.

## 4.1.4    A Recipe for Treatment

What are the key components necessary for successful treatment?

**Clinical Pearl**
**Key Components for Successful Treatment**

- Promoting successful weight gain
- Dealing with dysfunctional thoughts
- Regulating mood
- Addressing interpersonal difficulties
- Enhancing self-esteem
- Reducing over-concern with body shape

### Promoting Successful Weight Gain

*The golden rule in promoting weight gain is establishing a weight range rather than a set weight.* This helps to dispel the notion that there is a single absolute correct weight. In fact, this is a rather an imperfect science at best and one should aim for a weight within the normal healthy Body Mass Index range of 20–25 (Beumont et al., 1997). The amount of weight achieved per week should be in the range of 1–2 pounds. Our experience is that a dietitian, who is seen as credible and an expert in such matters, should prescribe the meal plan. In the absence of a dietitian, this can be done by the therapist. It should be borne in mind that patients will usually experience significant guilt in "going against the wishes of their AN" and eating, so it is best that these decisions initially be made by the clinician. It has also been suggested that patients be helped to see their meals as "medication" that will assist them in "inoculating" themselves against intense food cravings and thereby protect them from over-eating or bingeing (Garner et al., 1997).

An ideal weight range should be established, not a single set weight

The meal plan should comprise three main meals and at least two to three snacks. The therapist or dietitian needs to be cognizant of the fact that many patients with AN have been eating only minimal amounts of foods, and in such circumstances an initial energy intake of approximately 1,200 calories would be adequate. Less emaciated patients, or those who have been eating regular but smaller quantities of food, may consume the recommended normal energy intake for their age. Once minimal eating has been established, it is possible to make further dietary increases when the rate of weight gain slows down, as long as the patients are in fact completing each meal. It is important to adopt a collaborative approach with the patient, who may not necessarily agree with each calorific increase but still understand the justification for the increases. It has been our experience that most female patients will need an ultimate energy intake in excess of 3,000 calories per day to achieve full weight restoration.

**Clinical Pearl**
**Obstacles to Normal Eating**

In nearly all cases, the patient's digestive system is intact. The major challenges to the resumption of a normal pattern of eating are essentially behavioral and psychological. The problem is not so much managing the patient's diet, but rather dealing with obstacles that prevent the patient from following her meal plan. In a nutshell, prescribing the diet is relatively easy, but ensuring compliance is a different matter.

**Getting the patient to start eating again**

The first task is to get the patient to commence eating again and to gain weight at a consistent rate. The therapist should not become overzealous in encouraging too rapid a weight gain as this can result in a refeeding syndrome (see Section 4.1.5) that can be fatal. Although it may be cost effective to accelerate weight gain, this should always be balanced by the clinical disadvantages of doing so (Bemis, 1987). The risk of developing bulimic symptoms under such circumstances should not be underestimated. On the other hand, should the patient continue to lose weight, and especially if this is likely to place her in a life-threatening position, this would need to be urgently addressed.

Once the patient has begun to eat again, it is time to introduce the complex issue of forbidden foods. Dietitians usually report that when they ask their patients to produce a list of forbidden foods, the list by far exceeds what they are able to eat. The stage is therefore set for an interesting challenge. Most patients

**Many patients will not eat meat**

insist on being vegetarian – usually they mean that they don't eat red meat but

**Clinical Vignette**
**Confronting Weight Loss**

Therapist: Anna, you have lost more than 6 pounds over the last 3 weeks.
Anna:      Why are you making such a fuss about this, as I'm dealing with such important emotional issues, such as my anger towards my parents. How can you expect me to gain weight when I'm so upset?
Therapist: I'm bound by my professional obligations and laws of the state to try to protect you from harm, even self-harm. If you become seriously ill or actually died, I could be held legally responsible for your death. Do you want this to happen? I need you to help me to prevent this.

are willing to consume small quantities of white chicken or grilled fish. Our research has shown that true vegetarianism is relatively rare in our patients, and we allow patients to continue a vegetarian diet if there is evidence to show they were vegetarians prior to their developing an eating disorder (O'Connor, Touyz, Dunn, & Beumont, 1987). Most AN patients avoid red meat because of the fat content. An example of how patients with AN can challenge a dietitian with respect to their "taboo" or "forbidden" foods is illustrated in the clinical vignette below.

---

**Clinical Vignette**
**Refusal to Eat Dairy Products**

Patient:    I am allergic to dairy products, and if I eat them I will become extremely ill.

Therapist: How do you know it is the dairy products?

Patient:    Before I came to see you, I told my doctor that I felt nauseous whenever I ate dairy products. She advised me to stay away from them. My mother agrees with her. Why don't you ask her? She will tell you.

Therapist: Did the doctor do any special tests or send you to an allergist, a specialist physician who is best to advise on such matters?

Patient:    No

Therapist: Although some people are allergic to dairy products, most are not. As the avoidance of all such products will clearly complicate your treatment, it is important that we obtain an independent specialist opinion. Would you mind seeing a allergist? If she agrees, we will ensure that you have no dairy products in your diet.

Patient:    That's fine. Would you please discuss this with my mother?

---

## Binge-Eating and Vomiting

Self-monitoring sheets detailing the patient's food consumption, which are usually completed with obsessive detail in the patients with AN, should provide the therapist with a wealth of important material upon which to focus in therapy sessions and generate homework assignments. When the homework has not been successfully completed, the task is to identify and challenge the cognitive distortions that may have prevented the patient from complying with the assignment.

**Self-monitoring records of food consumption provide therapeutic material**

It is important to stress the relation between severe dietary restraint and the subsequent risk of binge eating and purging. The chart of the binge-purge cycle (Figure 1, Section 2.1) should be completed by the patient in the presence of the therapist. The therapist should also explore the ways that this cycle assists the patient in coping with feelings of distress and anxiety. The therapist can suggest the need to explore more adaptive ways of modulating mood. If asked, patients can usually describe an instance in which they were able to avoid the desire to binge or vomit because they were distracted by something that transpired. This is grist for the therapeutic mill, as it provides evidence to show the patients that they can in fact resist bingeing or purging, albeit infrequently. Their belief that they are simply unable to do so is therefore challenged. The therapist then works with the patient to develop alternative strategies to bingeing and/or vomiting that can be implemented almost immediately and that can delay the urge to binge. However, it is important to develop realistic strategies in order for this to succeed. There would be little point in deciding upon a 30 minute spa bath if the patient only had a shower in her home.

## Dealing with Dysfunctional Thoughts

Despite AN patients' reluctance to engage in treatment, they are often suffering greatly from intense feelings of coldness, hunger, constipation, lethargy, restlessness, and insomnia. As Garner et al. (1997) so aptly put it, "… symptoms are often intended to further the attainment of laudable goals, whereas on another level they represent adaptive failure" (p. 192). The clinician needs to establish a collaborative framework with the patient to identify and then explore underlying beliefs and assumptions that are contributing to the "adaptive failure." The diagnostic formulation which we have previously described can be used to target dysfunctional thoughts and processing errors. The first step is to familiarize the patient with the language skills necessary to master the basic principles of cognitive therapy. Once again, most clinicians would be familiar with these concepts, but the art here is to adapt them to the peculiarities of the AN patient.

**Underlying beliefs and assumptions need to be explored**

### Clinical Pearl
### Pitfalls in Teaching CBT Skills

We have consulted with numerous patients who present with both an impressive knowledge and the necessary clinical skills to suggest that they have mastered cognitive behavior therapy, but they have never been able to put it into practice. It should always be remembered that the aim is not to train a colleague for clinical practice but rather to impart the necessary knowledge and skills for the AN patient to overcome maladaptive thoughts and processing errors. It is fine for the patient to "talk the talk," but what is required is that she "walk the walk."

## Automatic Thoughts

**Automatic dysfunctional thoughts need to be identified**

Automatic thoughts can be adaptive, necessary, and valuable. For example, when experienced swimmers swimming in the ocean suddenly notice a very large wave approaching, they do not have to think consciously "I need to take a deep breath and then dive under the wave." This thought and the resulting behavior are simultaneous and automatic. However, not all automatic thoughts are adaptive or valid. CBT is useful not only for developing an understanding about how these thoughts become so firmly set in the patient's mind, but more importantly for how dysfunctional they are within the patient's daily world. It is extremely helpful for patients to identify automatic dysfunctional thoughts in their own lives as this emphasizes the importance that such thoughts play in maintaining their illness. Showing the patient that what goes through her mind can be identified, challenged, and corrected, and how this can then influence actual behaviors, provides a good framework for understanding learning principles. A good starting point for this is the dysfunctional thought record (DTR).

## Dysfunctional Thought Record (DTR)

The essence of CBT is to connect thoughts, emotions, and behaviors to provide an illustration to the patient as to why she feels or behaves in a particular

| Situation | Feelings | Dysfunctional Thoughts | Challenges Dysfunctional Thought(s) |
|---|---|---|---|
| Gary came up to me and asked me to go out on a date. | I always felt attached to him because he was so good looking and such a nice guy. | His favorite girl-friend must be out of town. He is only going to use me. Why would such a nice guy want with a fat and unattractive woman like myself? | Useful challenges to undertake in a situation such as this<br><br>a) What is the evidence for and against this?<br><br>b) Can these thoughts be reframed in any other way?<br><br>c) What are the likely consequences if I persist with these thoughts? |

**Figure 4**
**An Example of a Dysfunctional Thought Record (DTR)**

way in response to a specific event or circumstance. Once these dysfunctional thoughts have been identified, they can then be challenged so as to develop more adaptive and functional methods of coping. An example of a DTR is presented in Figure 4 below.

It cannot be overstated how important the contribution of regular homework is in the eventual successful completion of CBT. The worst mistake that any clinician can make is to ask the patient to complete DTRs on a daily basis and then to forget to ask for these or not to give them the attention that they deserve within the session. This is the bricks and mortar upon which the framework of CBT is based. If you don't value the homework assignments, neither will the patient.

## Cognitive Schemas

Cognitive schemas have been described as "enduring cognitive structures or sets that function by processing, organizing, and integrating complex information" (Garner et al., 1997, p. 122). In patients with AN, their illness becomes all-encompassing and represents their entire being. It is not at all uncommon for the AN patient to describe herself as "an anorectic" – rather than Jenny with an AN illness – and this reflects the pervasive nature of this disorder. It is sometimes helpful to ask a patient to draw a pie chart to illustrate the extent to which her eating disorder schema dominates her life. This is often a revealing exercise for the patient, especially when it is undertaken in a collaborative manner with the therapist.

For those clinicians not experienced in schema-based models, there are many excellent sources of information and detail (e.g., Garner et al., 1997; Hill & Touyz, 2007; Pike et al., 2005; Vitousek & Hollon, 1990; Young, Klosko, & Weishaar, 2003).

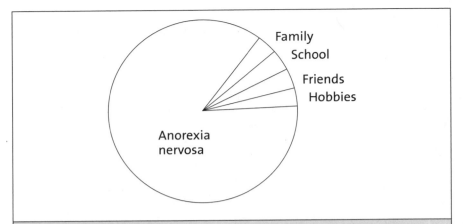

**Figure 5**
**Pie chart illustrating the extent to which AN is dominating the patient's life to the detriment of everything else.**

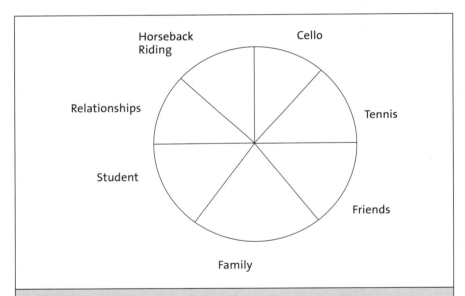

**Figure 6**
**Pie chart illustrating a much more healthy and diverse approach to life. "I am not an "anorectic," but instead a college student with family and friends, a relationship and hobbies.**

### Regulating Mood

**EDs often co-occur with anxiety disorders**

Current research indicates that eating disorders and anxiety disorders often co-occur and that the anxiety disorder usually predates the development of an eating disorder. As so often happens in such comorbid cases, the focus of attention often is on the eating disorder alone and not the anxiety disorder. In fact, it is even likely that the anxiety is completely overlooked when the initial history is taken. However, once anxiety is identified, the astute clinician needs to incorporate evidence-based treatment for the anxiety disorder that has been diagnosed along with the eating disorder treatment.

It is not uncommon for patients with AN to become depressed, especially when they have lost weight. Medication has only a limited role to play (see Section 4.4). Many patients report that their depression is ameliorated considerably with weight gain but this is not always the case. Specific CBT modules addressing dysphoria can easily incorporated into treatment.

Fairburn et al. (2003) have described what they call "mood intolerance." What they mean by this is that the patient is unable to adequately deal with certain mood states, including positive ones such as excitement. Instead of acknowledging fluctuations in their mood and handling these in an appropriate manner, patients employ "dysfunctional mood modulatory behavior." As the authors point out, this diminishes their ability to identify what might have triggered the mood state. It also serves a further function of neutralizing the affect, but this occurs to the detriment of the patient. Dysfunctional mood modulatory behavior is exhibited in different ways such as:

- Self-injurious behavior (cutting, burning, scratching or even head banging).
- Psychoactive substances (alcohol, psychoactive drugs, illicit drugs).
- Excessive exercise, self-induced vomiting ,or bingeing.

Although the more traditional CBT techniques may have a role to play in such cases, additional strategies are called for that have been specifically developed to deal with mood intolerance. Such strategies can be found in dialectical behavior therapy (DBT; Linehan, 1993) or in mindfulness-based CBT for depression (Segal, Williams, & Teasdale, 2002).

## Addressing Interpersonal Difficulties

Although the nature of the symptoms of AN is fairly consistent across patients, each patient is a unique individual with her own constellation of family, friends, and acquaintances. Family therapy is usually indicated for younger patients with AN, especially those still attending school. It is important to understand exactly how interpersonal processes (family related or otherwise) contribute to maintaining mechanisms in AN. The significance of this is well illustrated in the following clinical vignette of a 15-year-old girl who was receiving treatment in an eating disorder unit.

**Each patient is unique**

### Clinical Vignette
#### Addressing Interpersonal Processes

Therapist: You seem pretty determined to hold onto your illness at any cost.
Patient: Why should you care? I suppose you say that to all your patients. In my case, I really have no choice.
Therapist: I would like to challenge your last statement. We have already looked at the cost of maintaining your illness on both your health and your general well-being. If I remember correctly, you agreed with me that it was a high price to pay.
Patient: You don't seem to understand. I really have no choice in the matter. Let's forget about it.
Therapist: Why don't you give me the benefit of the doubt?
Patient: OK then, if I get over this, my parents will get divorced and it will be all my fault.
Therapist: How can that be? I don't understand.

**Clinical Vignette**
**(Continued)**

Patient:    One night when my parents thought I was asleep, I overheard them whispering in their bedroom. My parents agreed to stay together until I got better – then they would divorce. Their marriage is really bad. So you can now see that if I get better, I mess up my parent's marriage for good. It will be all my fault.
Therapist:  It is extremely helpful for you to have told me this. Thank you.

This clinical vignette speaks for itself. Similar situations where interpersonal processes maintain the illness occur in situations where more than one member of a family (or a close friend) has AN. A common scenario is having two close family members competing with one another (usually mother and daughter) to see who can eat the least at every meal. Long-term interpersonal difficulties can also have an adverse impact on self-esteem, thereby increasing the need to pursue other desirable goals such as controlling eating, weight, and shape (Fairburn et al., 2003).

A different kind of interpersonal problem is also frequently present in AN patients. AN usually occurs during those vital years of adolescence when psychosexual development is crucial. Unfortunately, many patients with AN are ill for most of these crucial years and although they may have a chronological age of 20, they may have never attended dance parties, been out on a date, or even held hands with a member of the opposite sex. Overcoming their AN means that they now expected to engage in age-appropriate social activities for which they are ill equipped. To put it more bluntly, they lack the basic social skills to successfully engage in interpersonal relationships, and they are terrified. It is imperative for the clinician to remain cognizant of this and not encourage the patient to embark on a task for which she is not ready. This would simply reinforce the patient's sense of failure and once again increase the pressure to control eating, weight, and shape. It has been our experience that a great deal of planning needs to go into preparing for each new social event. Role playing makes an important contribution here. Afterward each event needs to be thoroughly reviewed, with the successes reinforced and any failures carefully analyzed to determine what might have gone wrong. Although the clinician may feel that the therapeutic endeavor is complete once the patient has resumed eating normally and attained a healthy weight, much more work often needs to be done. As one AN patient once put it "I am now an AN patient at normal weight – I am not sure whether I am better or worse off."

It has been our experience that day hospital programs can be extremely helpful for such patients as they have to learn to engage with peers on a daily basis. This is particularly valuable, as by this time many in the group are engaging in healthy social interactions from which the patient can learn while slowly gaining confidence. Most of us have families, live in communities, attend school, university, or work, and our interpersonal relationships play a vital role in our overall well-being. Unfortunately, those with chronic AN live a reclusive lifestyle with a very much reduced quality of life. By this stage, they will have probably not eaten socially for years, and any improvement is unlikely. This point was hammered home to one of the authors who arrived at

> **Patients with AN have lost out on years of social development**

---

**Clinical Vignette**

**Taking that First Step (16-Year-Old with AN)**

| | |
|---|---|
| Therapist: | What do you think you will be doing this weekend? |
| Patient: | I'll be home with my family. |
| Therapist: | Wouldn't you like to meet up with your friends? |
| Patient: | I suppose so, but I really couldn't be bothered. They like to go to parties and be with boys, and I would feel left out. |
| Therapist: | How about I ask your mother to invite friends of theirs over who have a daughter of your age. That way, they can take the responsibility for the arrangements and you can see your friend. |
| Patient: | I suppose. |

---

a day hospital at lunch time to find six chronic AN patients sitting by themselves, each under a separate tree, struggling to eat their lunch only yards apart – yet there was absolutely no social interaction.

As Treasure (1997) points out, it may seem inappropriate for a parent to take care of their 16-year-old's social life, but someone needs to take the initiative to get things going. Enlisting the support of the family – with the consent of your patient – could result in kick-starting her social life.

## Enhancing Self-Esteem

The treatment of core low self-esteem in patients with ED's is now receiving the attention it deserves. Fairburn and colleagues have drawn attention to the importance of "core low self-esteem" as a maintaining mechanism in patients with BN (Fairburn et al., 2003). This is very much the case for patients with AN in whom long-standing poor self-esteem has often become part of the patient's identity.

*Low core self-esteem needs to be dealt with*

For clinicians not experienced in treating patients with AN, the history obtained would appear to contradict the notion that such patients could possibly have such a low "core self-esteem." The patient's achievements seem never-ending (e.g., leader at school, top athlete, or class president). In fact, these patients typically appear to have excelled in every endeavor in which they have participated. However, nothing could be further from the truth, as such perfectionism comes with a significant cost.

One would therefore expect that there would be a considerable literature describing how best to deal with this "low core self-esteem" in AN, but surprisingly this is not the case. However, there are many excellent workbooks on the subject of low self-esteem which are easily adaptable for use with AN patients (e.g., Fennell, 1999; McKay & Fanning, 1992).

---

**Clinical Vignette**

**Challenging Self-Worth**

| | |
|---|---|
| Patient: | I am petrified that I won't be able to maintain my high distinction grades in my examinations this semester. |
| Therapist: | What would be your understanding if you failed to live up to this goal? |
| Patient: | This would clearly indicate that I am a total failure and therefore a worthless individual. |

**Clinical Vignette**
**(Continued)**

Therapist: Are you actually telling me that you evaluate your worth by maintaining a distinction average.

Patient: Could there be any other way? You simply have to excel in anything you undertake. No compromise is possible. It doesn't really matter whether it is one's college grades, or sports, or even hobbies or a relationship with one's friends. I started to feel more in control when I began to lose weight this semester.

Therapist: The way you choose to equate self-worth raises some interesting issues. Do you think that scientists would evaluate self-worth on how someone executes their tasks on a day by day basis like you do?

Patient: Doesn't everyone determine their self-worth by their accomplishments?

Therapist: We may well do so to some extent but not nearly in the critical manner that you appear to do and definitely not on an hour-to-hour basis. Do you evaluate your peer's self-worth by their accomplishments? You mentioned your friend Kate – do you rate her worth on the grades she attained this semester? And by the way, you haven't seemed particularly interested in how well I performed during my clinical training.

Patient: I took it for granted that you excelled in everything you did.

Therapist: I can assure you that is not the case – take my golf handicap of 27 as an example. Would your evaluation of me change if you now know that I am not particularly good golfer? I can assure you that a golf handicap of 27 is nothing to write home about.

Patient: Not really. After all you are a professor.

Adapted from Garner et al., 1997, p 129

Finally, eating disorder patients believe that there is only one route by which they can improve their self-esteem, and that is by enhancing the way they look. As Rosen (1997) points out, "dieting and exercise are viewed as the main beauty remedies." However, patients really need to accept that, unlike a failed marriage in which divorce is a possibility, they cannot disengage themselves from their bodies. The only reasonable alterative is to compromise and become more accepting in this regard, defects and all (Cash, 1995).

### Reducing Over-Concern with Body Shape

Since the 1970s, there has been an avalanche of information regarding the assessment, pathology, and the development of body image (Rosen, 1997). However, despite Bruch's assertion that the "correction of body shape misperception is a precondition to recovery," there is almost no literature on how this is best achieved (Delinsky & Wilson, 2006; Farrell, Shafran, & Lee, 2006).

*Addressing body-shape concern*

Dysfunctional shape concerns are an essential diagnostic criterion for AN and BN, but clinicians fail to give this symptom the prominence it deserves. Although much attention is given to improving eating behavior, reinforcing weight gain, and/or reducing overactivity (Touyz, Lennerts, Arthur, & Beumont 1993), endeavoring to reduce body shape concern is often left to the end of sessions rather than taking center stage in therapy. We have found that such concerns can linger on and continue to cause significant distress long after the patient has gained weight (Windauer, Lennerts, Talbot, Touyz, & Beumont, 1993).

So when confronted by dysfunctional shape concerns, where do you begin? Fairburn (in press) provides some prudent advice on this matter. Parsimony is the order of the day. Start with simple, well-established techniques and don't try to do too much at once. It is imperative to do a few things well rather than using a smorgasbord of strategies badly.

There are two major guiding principles to assist patients with AN to overcome their dysfunctional weight and shape concerns. The first is to educate the patients to enable them to recognize how these concerns have come to dominate their daily lives. Once this has been achieved, it is time to introduce both cognitive restructuring and behavioral strategies to reduce both the intensity and frequency of ritualistic behaviors. A point worth documenting here is that we do live in a society that remains enamored of scrawny fashion models and actresses, and the patient's concerns about being fat in contrast to such images need to be dealt with in an honest fashion. Her views about this must be acknowledged because they are real. Any attempt to dismiss these beliefs will diminish your credibility.

## Body Shape Education

Rosen (1997) places great value on educating AN patients about the concept of body shape and how over-concerns about it arise. This can be achieved by a multimedia presentation integrating mini-tutorials, interactive debate, and the use of homework assignments, including audiotape sessions and self-help books (Cash, 1991, 1995). In this instance, more appears to be better. Rosen also finds it helpful for the AN patient to document a brief history of her own body image as well as any factors that may have influenced it. This includes their early childhood (up to age 7), later childhood, early adolescence, teenage years, and early adulthood as well as the present. Both positive and negative influences should be reported. Remember that any earlier distress pertaining to body shape can be triggered at a later stage.

The final stage of this education process is to draw attention to both the nature and extent of dysfunctional shape and weight concerns and what impact these have on daily life. This is achieved by means of a body-checking monitoring sheet (not dissimilar to the one used to document eating behavior). Often patients are oblivious to how common and disabling these body-checking behaviors are (Fairburn, in press). The monitoring sheet should have sufficient columns to record the time, place, the checking behavior, any identified trigger, as well as any cognitions or feelings prior to and following the checking behavior. Such information proves invaluable in deciding which behaviors to stop, reduce, or modify. It is also worthwhile to document any avoidance behaviors as patients will need to be encouraged to undertake behavioral experiments to expose themselves gradually to the avoided activity. Fairburn also sees value in addressing "feelings of fatness." The patients are asked to document the times when they experience strong feelings of fatness and any feelings or associations that are connected with it such as feelings of boredom, depression, tiredness, or when their clothes are feeling too tight. Most patients will be astounded at both the extent of their checking behaviors and the amount of time that they spend agonizing over feelings of fatness with the associated negative mood state that invariably follows.

**Patients need to be made aware of their body-checking behaviors**

The stage is now set to commence cognitive restructuring and introduce behavioral strategies to deal with body checking behaviors such as weighing oneself repeatedly, inspecting any imperfection in the mirror, or participating in grooming rituals (Rosen, 1997).

## Cognitive Restructuring

The clinician should now have ample data with which to undertake cognitive restructuring. As Rosen (1997) points out, traditional techniques used in the treatment of anxiety and depression work well when using cognitive restructuring to treat patients with eating disorders. The patient is asked to provide evidence for and against a maladaptive belief; the evidence offered is as important as the belief itself.

---

**Clinical Vignette**
**Cognitive Restructuring**

Patient:    There is no way I could ever go to the beach as I would not be seen dead in a bathing suit (even if all my friends went).
Therapist:  Why would this be so? What would stop you?
Patient:    Just imagine me (Ms. Waddle) waddling down to the edge of the ocean to have a swim. Everyone on the crowded beach would be asking themselves why such a fat slob would dare to expose herself in a bathing suit. They would all laugh and I would be beside myself choking with embarrassment.
Therapist:  Are you really saying that you honestly believe that everyone on that crowded beach would take the trouble to single you out and watch every move you made. They would stop their conversations, cease reading, or stop eating their lunch and focus their entire attention on you – I hadn't realized how important you were.
Patient:    When you say it like that, I guess not. I'm not Angelina Jolie.
Therapist:  When you talk to yourself like this, how does it make you feel?
Patient:    Terrible... that I am fat, ugly, and unattractive and that I will never have a boyfriend.
Therapist:  So maybe you should ease up on yourself a bit. Do you believe that no other woman on the beach might feel a little self-conscious about her figure?
Patient:    I guess so.

---

The clinician needs to assist the patient with reducing negative self-talk and developing a list of more positive self-statements, which should be memorized and available whenever the need arises.

**A courtroom scenario may help patients change irrational cognitions**

Another strategy that could prove useful is the courtroom scenario described by Treasure (1997). The clinician plays the role of a prosecutor who is determined to obtain a conviction. The accused is a Ms. Anna-Rexic, who is charged with being too fat. Your patient is asked to defend her and to ensure that the jury returns a "not guilty" verdict.

Prosecutor: Members of the jury, I contend that Ms. Anna-Rexic is so fat that she is now denied the opportunity to fly overseas on holiday using a low-cost airline. She simply can't fit into the seat. Isn't that overwhelming evidence that she is fat?

Patient (as Defense Lawyer): This is simply not the case. There is ample evidence to suggest that she is not fat. My client takes the bus home from school each day and sits in exactly the same size seat as would be found on a low-cost aircraft. She can't possibly be as fat as you claim she is.

The clinician and patient can pool their creative talents to continue this script. It should be grossly exaggerated so that the patient is able to laugh with the clinician about how farcical and absurd this issue is. The patient could then be encouraged to visit an art gallery where it will quickly become apparent that plumpness was once a desired quality. They can then compare this to contemporary society where thinness is idealized. It also is helpful to get rid of fashion magazines at home; one of Treasure's (1997) patients called these "anorexia porn."

Not all AN patients admit to a preoccupation with weight and/or shape or feelings of intense body dissatisfaction. These issues become particularly challenging when AN patients start to regain weight. The patient needs to be prepared to effectively challenge her dysfunctional concerns as they arise.

Finally, as we have stated previously, it is not possible for the patient to divorce herself from her body, she will usually have to learn to live with imperfections in her body.

---

**Clinical Pearl**
**The Levi's Principle**

---

Patients with AN believe that their weights are governed by the Levi's Principle, i.e., that (j)eans rather than (g)enes determine their weight. Treasure (1997) encourages her patients to shop at a clothing store that allows you to return clothes that don't fit. She encourages them to get some size 16 clothes (the average size of a British woman). The clinician then explores with the patient what conclusions she should come to when she tries on these larger clothes and question whether she still believes that she is actually bigger than average.

## Behavioral Strategies

Rosen (1997) has documented several behavioral strategies that can be used effectively to deal with dysfunctional body shape concerns, especially body-checking behavior. These comprise exposure to avoided situations response prevention of checking and grooming, reassurance seeking, comparing, and adopting pleasurable bodily experiences.

## Exposure to Avoided Situations

Prior to confronting any anxiety-provoking situations outside the home, the patient should undertake exercises to reduce her overconcern with her own body. Rosen (1997) suggests that a hierarchy be constructed that encompasses both the most satisfying as well as most distressing body parts. The patient uses the privacy of her own home to stand in front of a full length mirror to work through each step of the hierarchy. One or two minutes are spent on each step, and the process is initially undertaken with the patient fully clothed. Once this has been satisfactorily negotiated, the patient may confront her unclothed body. Some patients may find the use of progressive muscle relaxation helpful

**Encourage the patient to confront her body in a mirror**

(Rosen, 1997). We have recently described the use of mirror exposure as an adjunct to treatment in a day hospital setting for patients with eating disorders (Taylor, Touyz, George, Thornton, & Beumont, 2005).

The wealth of data obtained from the body checking and avoidance monitoring sheets should prove to be invaluable. Specific situations, such as avoiding the beach, as described in a previous vignette, can be discussed and analyzed. Other avoidant behaviors which can be addressed include wearing tighter fitting clothes instead of baggy ones and removing hair from the face if it is deliberately covering any blemish. There are many others.

### Response Prevention of Checking and Grooming

Patients engage in multiple body checking and grooming behaviors. These will once again become apparent when reviewing the self monitoring sheets. Checking behavior includes constantly measuring oneself with a tape measure, using ones fingers to measure wrist size, pinching the skin, constantly checking for blemishes in the mirror. Constant grooming behavior is also evident. It is not uncommon for such patients to try on several different outfits before they literally force themselves out of the house. The clinician works closely with the patient to determine which behaviors should cease immediately and those that need to be reduced or modified (see Rosen, 1997).

### Reassurance Seeking

Patients with AN are known to constantly seek reassurance from others by demanding to know whether any imperfection is still noticeable or has become more prominent. Parents, relatives, and friends often become exasperated by this relentless onslaught, not knowing where to turn. Rosen (1997) has described this behavior clearly:

> This behavior is another example of negative body talk, except that it is verbalized aloud to others. Reassurance seeking is self-defeating because it does not eliminate the preoccupation (the patient does not believe the reassurance); it inadvertently trains other people to take even more interest in the patient's appearance; and it can strain relationships with partners and family members. (p. 197)

Reassurance seeking behavior needs to be identified and eliminated at the first available opportunity.

### Comparing

Patients constantly compare themselves to the world's most beautiful models and actresses. Focusing attention on such photographs or images only ends up with the patient accentuating any imperfection that she might have and then devaluing herself. The problem that needs to be faced here is that the comparison is an unfair one. She is not comparing herself to her peers, but to the most beautiful women in the mass media, whose appearances have often been digitally altered to enhance their beauty. The patient is asked to stop comparing herself to others. She is asked instead to illuminate what she finds attractive in other women, as well as pointing out any imperfections in them. The challenge here is to end up with a much more realistic appraisal.

**Pleasurable Body Experiences**

Vandereycken, Probst, and van Bellinghen and colleagues (1992) drew attention to the importance of patients getting into touch with their bodies through dance, massage, and sensory awareness exercises. Patients also can be encouraged to have a spa bath or manicure/pedicure. All these activities have the desired goal of enabling patients "to experience their bodies as a pleasurable instrument." Rosen (1997) makes the good point that such activities would actually encompass a two-fold objective in that they double-up as an exposure activity as well.

## 4.1.5 Family Therapy in Adolescents and Children with Anorexia Nervosa

Family therapy is regarded as an integral part of treatment for adolescents and children with AN – this is a far cry from Gull's advice in the nineteenth century to separate the sufferer from her family!

**Including family of the patient in therapy is important**

A variety of family therapies have been evaluated based on family systems theory. These include strategic, structural and the Milan approaches (Lock & le Grange, 2005). Other approaches include "family group psycho-education," (in which families are seen together in a class format), conjoint family therapy and "separated" family therapy (in which patients and parents are seen separately), behavioral family systems therapy (wherein parents, as in the Maudsley approach, are encouraged to take responsibility for refeeding their children, with the addition of specific training in communication and problem skills after the refeeding period), and, finally, a form of structural family therapy, with and without individual body-awareness therapy (focusing on correcting distorted body image).

Family approaches thus take several forms, but the one with best evidence is the Maudsley model with more recent variants of family counseling (Lock, le Grange, Agras, & Dare, 2001). The Maudsley approach has three specific phases; the first focuses on refeeding the patient and includes a family meal; the second focuses on negotiations for a new pattern of relationships; and the third entails the establishment of a healthy adolescent or young adult relationship with the parents, in which the disordered eating does not constitute the basis of interaction. This includes working towards increased personal autonomy for the adolescent.

With all approaches, it is important to engage the family in the therapy and in order to do this, an interview of the family, including everyone living in the home, is arranged at an early stage. If separated, both parents are still encouraged to attend. The meeting is held on the premise that members are concerned and want to do their best to help each other. Guilt is common and families can be advised that this is a futile emotion and that no family is perfect. Families should be reassured that having a member with AN can disrupt any family, even the most robust. Family members, including siblings, are encouraged to share their feelings. Anger is often felt, and interpreted as an expression of concern.

At the first session the clinician evaluates the family's strengths and weaknesses, and ensures that a positive comment is conveyed to each member as the session closes. In the case of emergent major problems such as physical or sexual abuse, substance abuse, or difficulties with another child (e.g., substance abuse or disturbed behavior), the family is referred to a specialist therapist. However, such associated psychopathology is uncommon. Most families, or at least the parents, are offered regular sessions, with the aim being to elicit the family's assistance in helping the member with AN. Although this was developed for adolescent patients, this approach can be adapted for older patients by bringing in the spouse and other family members.

**Dieticians can teach the patient and family about healthy eating**

*Dietary advice.* Because the patient's eating must be addressed, a dietician is a critical member of the treatment team who can evaluate the food eaten, its energy value, and whether the diet includes essential nutrients. The patient and family are taught about normal healthy eating. Many patients believe that 1,000 calories a day is sufficient. Actually, twice as much energy consumption is necessary to maintain healthy body weight, but consumption should be increased gradually. The patient with an eating disorder is likely to be in negative energy balance and needs to eat more than normal in order to regain healthy nutritional status. Although the Lock et al. (2001) manual does not advocate utilizing specific dietary advice other than to eat nourishing foods, we believe that it is essential to address this issue directly, and that this providing advice about nutrition is crucial to prevent refeeding syndrome, which can be fatal.

In inpatient programs, patients are encouraged to rest after eating. Some programs also recommend warming at this time, e.g., increasing the temperature of the room. This practice is based on animal studies showing decreased activity levels with warming.

**Refeeding too aggressively can be dangerous**

Patients can become very ill, even die, with rapid renutrition, precipitating a "refeeding syndrome." This occurs when metabolism is stimulated by the sudden introduction of larger amounts of food, launching a demand for substances like potassium and phosphates within the body's cells, and, given the depletion of reserves due to the prior starvation/dieting, this can be met only by drastically reducing plasma levels. Features of the syndrome include cardiac failure, shortness of breath, weakness, edema, seizures, delirium, and coma. Therapists thus need to realize that patients can be in more danger when they start to get better and refeed than they were at the nadir of their reduced weight.

---

**Clinical Pearl**
**It's Wise to Use a Dietician**

---

Most clinicians working in the field of eating disorders have had little or no training in nutrition. Although patients with eating disorders usually give the impression that they are extremely knowledgeable in this area, they are often misinformed or have distorted views about caloric values and the effects of eating particular foods. A dietician knowledgeable about eating disorders is in the best position to provide nutritional counseling. Patients are more likely to trust the information coming from such experts, so it is a good idea to send the patient for a consultation with such a practitioner.

---

Weekly reviews with the therapist are necessary until substantial improvement in the patient's physical and psychological state is achieved. Weight should be recorded on each occasion. Family members can be encouraged to help to monitor progress. Although eating does improve gradually, increased intake has to be maintained. It is not enough for patients to stop losing weight; increased intake has to be monitored so that weight can be regained at the rate of about one pound per week. Those clinicians who wish to use an evidence-based manual to conduct this treatment can refer to Lock, et al. (2001).

**Clinical Pearl**
**The Key to Successful Psychotherapy**

The key to successful psychotherapy in AN is a blend of care and concern, showing genuine interest, promoting autonomy, and firmly insisting that the patient will not be allowed to starve. Criticism is best avoided; instead, praise is given when appropriate. Patients with AN usually have a vulnerable sense of self and low self-esteem that can be adversely affected by denigrating or punitive therapeutic approaches. On the other hand, patients need to trust that the therapist will not abandon them. (See section 5.1 for a relevant vignette)

## 4.2 Mechanism of Action

### 4.2.1 Psychodynamic and Related Therapies

Psychodynamic therapies have the longest history in therapies for eating disorders. They have developed from open-ended to more time-limited structured approaches (Dare & Crowther, 1995). A key figure in the application of such therapies in AN was Bruch (1973) (see Chapter 2). She described two core therapeutic elements of change in AN: (a) developing an understanding of the meaning of food for the patient, and (b) helping her to find alternatives to anorexic self-experience and self-expression.

Psychodynamic therapies are long-term and demand a considerable commitment of time, energy, and money. They also require specific training that may not be readily accessible or available. Dare and Crowther (1995) have developed focal psychoanalytic therapy (FPT) for AN as a standardized form of time-limited psychoanalytic therapy that may be more readily accessible and disseminated, and subject to empirical evaluation. The therapist takes a nondirective stance, gives no advice about the eating behaviors or other problems of symptom management, but addresses first the unconscious and conscious meanings of the symptom in terms of the patient's history and family experiences. Next the effects of the symptom and its influence on current interpersonal relationships are explored, and finally, the manifestation of those influences in the patient's relationship with the therapist is analyzed. A nondirective stance can, however, present challenges in child and adolescent treatment settings given parental pressure for a cure, and pediatricians' expectation of active interventions.

> Psychodynamic therapies are long-term

Self-psychology for eating disorders such as BN (Goodsitt, 1997) developed out of the older psychodynamic traditions, and it approaches BN as a specific case of the pathology of the self. Patients cannot rely on people to fulfill their needs, particularly needs such as self-esteem. Eating disordered patients rely instead on a substance, food, to fulfill personal needs. Therapy progresses when patients begin to rely on other people in their lives, starting with the therapist.

*Unfortunately* there is little evidence to support these approaches (Hay & Bacaltchuk, 2006; Treasure & Schmidt, 2005). A single randomized controlled trial of focal psychoanalytic therapy found it to be as effective as other psychotherapies in outpatient treatment of anorexia nervosa, but outcomes were poor in the majority of participants in all groups (see Section 4.3.1 below).

## 4.2.2    Cognitive Behavior, Cognitive, and Behavior Therapies

**CBT, CT, and BT**
**are time-limited**
**therapies**

Cognitive behavior therapy (CBT), cognitive therapy (CT), and behavior therapy (BT) are time-limited manual-based therapies that address abnormal cognitions (beliefs) and behaviors thought to promote and maintain the disorder. Garner and colleagues (1997) describe CBT for AN as a therapy that addresses patients' beliefs, attitudes, and assumptions about the meaning of body weight. Thinness is seen as the principal avenue to self-worth and weight gain is feared. Combinations of positive and negative reinforcers maintain the patient's behavior and help explain the ego-syntonic nature of the illness. Strategies that challenge these beliefs and behaviors in order to normalize eating patterns are promoted.

Fairburn and colleagues (2003) have recently developed an alternate CBT approach, modelled on CBT for BN (see above) that addresses four key illness-maintaining factors. These are clinical perfectionism, low self-esteem, mood intolerance, and interpersonal difficulties. Strategies derived from dialectical behavior therapy and interpersonal psychotherapy are incorporated to help address these additional aspects. Fairburn et al. note that this approach is not inconsistent with the involvement of the family for the treatment of young patients. Forms of CBT have also been evaluated in posthospitalisation trials in AN (e.g., Pike, Walsh, Vitousek, Wilson, & Bauer, 2003).

**Nonspecific clinical**
**management – a**
**recent nonspecific**
**therapy**

A more recent nonspecific therapy for AN that is less directive than earlier forms of CBT, while still including many behavioral elements, has been developed in New Zealand (McIntosh et al., 2005). It is called nonspecific clinical management (NSCM). NSCM includes psychoeducation, "care," and supportive psychotherapy, with a focus on resumption of normal eating and weight gain, strategies for weight maintenance, information about energy requirements, and relearning to eat normally. It thus incorporates elements of nutritional counseling and some behavioral weight restoration strategies. Treatment is relatively short, comprising 20 one-hour manual-based sessions over a minimum of 20 weeks. In one treatment trial results were promising, but many patients remained symptomatic, indicating that this approach might be a useful first phase in a longer-term therapy.

In BN, another variation that is sometimes used as a comparison therapy, is behavior therapy (BT). This involves applying behavioral strategies only, such as keeping a diary of eating patterns, a return to "normal" eating, and techniques to help distract the patient from extreme weight control behaviors such as vomiting. This approach has been found to be less effective than full CBT-BN (Fairburn et al., 1993).

In the 1980s, a modification of the exposure and response prevention therapy developed for obsessive compulsive disorder was developed for adults with BN. It involved exposure to food and then implementation of psychological prevention strategies of weight-control behavior, such as vomiting after eating, until the urge or compulsion to vomit receded (Carter, Bulik, McIntosh, & Joyce, 2002; Leitenberg, Rosen, Gross, Nudelman, & Vara, 1988). In RCTs evaluating its efficacy in enhancing the effectiveness of CBT-BN compared to a wait-list control, it was found to add little to the parent treatment (e.g., Agras, Schneider, Arnow, Raeburn, & Telch, 1989; also see Hay, Bacaltchuk, & Stefano, 2004, for a meta-analysis of this form of therapy). This approach has not gained widespread support.

Griffiths, Hadzi-Pavlovic, and Channon-Little (1996) have developed hypno-behavioral psychotherapy for BN. This uses a combination of behavioral techniques, such as self-monitoring to change maladaptive eating behaviors, and hypnotic techniques to reinforce and encourage behavior change. However, only a single short term RCT (Griffiths et al., 1996) has been conducted thus far.

There have been a number of other attempts to enhance CBT for BN but as yet none has widespread support. For example, microecological momentary assessment (EMA), an intensive monitoring schedule, did not significantly enhance self-monitoring in a small RCT (le Grange, Gorin, Dymek, & Stone, 2002). A more promising, but yet unproven, approach is Fairburn and colleagues' (2003) "transdiagnostic therapy" described above. Finally, many with BED are also overweight or obese, and adding strategies that help address their weight disorder, such as exercise, may be important to long-term outcome (see Pendleton, Goodrick, Poston, Reeves, & Foreyt, 2002).

## 4.2.3    Other "Behavioral" Therapies

Cognitive-analytic therapy (CAT) is a treatment that combines elements of CT and brief-focused psychodynamic therapy. CAT integrates active symptom management, and has been recommended as a viable alternative to CBT for AN (Garner & Needleman, 1997). Patients are helped to evolve a formal, mapped-out structure of the place of AN in their experience of themselves and their early and current relationships. This is drawn in diagrammatic form, and the figure may be modified over the course of the treatment (Treasure, Todd, Brolly, Tiller, Nehmed, & Deman, 1995). Treatment is conducted in 20 weekly sessions, with monthly "booster" sessions over three months. Therapists require specific training and supervision.

**CAT can be a viable alternative to CBT for patients with AN**

Cognitive orientation theory aims to generate a systematic procedure for exploring the thematic meaning of a behavior, such as avoidance of certain emotions. Therapy for modifying behavior focuses on systematically changing beliefs related to themes, not beliefs referring directly to eating behavior. No attempt is made to persuade patients that their beliefs are incorrect or maladaptive (Bachar, Yael, Shulamit, & Berry, 1999). This is however a little-used therapy with only one very small and inconclusive trial.

Finally, dialectical behavior therapy (DBT) is a type of behavioral therapy that views emotional dysregulation as the core problem in BN, with binge eating and purging understood as attempts to influence, change, or control painful emotional states. Patients are taught a repertoire of skills to replace dysfunctional behaviors (Safer, Telch, & Agras, 2001). While this is a promising approach there has only been one short term (20 week) RCT of its use in bulimia nervosa in 31 women. This trial found that DBT significantly increased cessation of binge eating or purging (28.6% abstinence) compared with patients in a waitlist control condition and significantly reduced bulimic symptom scores and dietary restraint scores compared with the waiting list control. There was no significant difference in depression scores between the DBT and the waiting list control (Hay et al., 2004). In addition, there has been one promising trial in 44 women with binge eating disorder (Safer, Lively, Telch, & Agras,

2002; Telch, Agras, & Linehan, 2001). However, although 89% of the women receiving DBT had stopped binge eating by the end of treatment only 56% were abstinent at the 6-month follow-up. Relapse was associated with higher restraint post treatment.

### 4.2.4    Interpersonal Psychotherapy

**IPT, first used to treat depression, has been modified for use with BN patients**

Interpersonal psychotherapy (IPT) was first developed for treatment of depression and was later modified for treatment of BN (Fairburn et al., 1991). Like CBT, it is a manual-based therapy and thus readily amenable to empirical evaluation. IPT uses three overlapping phases in the treatment of BN. The first phase analyses the interpersonal context of the eating disorder, leading to a formulation of the person's problem area(s), which then form the focus of the second phase. The third phase aims at monitoring progress in making interpersonal changes and exploring ways to cope with further interpersonal difficulties. In BN, but not necessarily in AN, the therapist does not attend to eating patterns or body attitudes.

Specific training is required for the successful delivery of IPT, and it is unclear how common IPTs use by therapists has become. It has been evaluated in longitudinal studies in comparison with CBT-BN. However, the results have been equivocal (McIntosh et al., 2005). Addressing interpersonal issues in therapy has empirical support, however, as disturbed relationships are known to be important factors in the maintenance of eating disorders (Fairburn et al., 2003; see Chapter 1). CBT-BN has been found to lead to symptomatic change earlier than IPT for people with BN (e.g., Agras, Crow, Halmi, Mitchell, Wilson, & Kraemer, 2000; Fairburn et al., 1991), but by one year follow-up, IPT was shown to be just as effective as CBT.

### 4.2.5    Feminist Therapy

Feminist therapy rests on the proposition that cultural constructions of gender are central to the understanding and treatment of eating disorders. Katzman and Lee (1997), Striegel-Moore (1995), and Wooley (1995) are key figures in the integration of feminist and transcultural approaches to eating disorders. Detailed descriptions of feminist therapy are found in Dolan and Gitzinger (1994). Although addressing feminist issues in therapy has "face validity" for a disorder in which 90% of sufferers are women with body image concerns, there are no RCTs evaluating its approach and it is unclear how widely it is used.

### 4.2.6    Motivational Enhancement Therapy

**MET targets the ego-syntonic nature of AN**

Vitousek, Watson, and Wilson (1998) and Ward, Troop, Todd, & Treasure (1996) have developed motivational enhancement therapies (METs) for EDs. This treatment targets the ego-syntonic nature of the illness and is based on a stages of change model. Stages of change represent constellations of intentions and behaviors through which individuals pass as they move from having a problem to doing something to resolve it. Patients in the *precontemplation* stage show no intention to change. Those in the *contemplation* acknowledge that they have a problem and are thinking about change, but have not yet made a commitment to change (Rieger et al., 2000). Patients in the third stage (*action*) are actively engaged in overcoming their problems, while those in *maintenance* work to prevent relapse. The aim of MET is to help patients to move from earlier stages into action, utilizing cognitive and emotional strategies. For example, with precontemplators, the therapist explores perceived positive and negative aspects of abnormal eating behaviors. Open-ended questions are used to elicit client expression, and reflective paraphrasing is used to reinforce key points of motivation (Miller and Rollnick, 2002). During a session following structured assessment, most of the time is devoted to explaining feedback about the assessment to the client. Therapy then progresses to developing and consolidating a change plan (Prochaska, DiClemente, & Norcross, 1992).

Motivational enhancement therapy is a widely used approach in psychiatry and psychology, and has applicability in AN where there is often strong resistance to change. As an approach, it would arguably be a useful adjunct to other specific therapies, but is as yet unsupported by evidence. We were only able to locate one relevant RCT, which compared four sessions of motivational enhancement therapy with CBT (Treasure, Katzman, & Schmidt, 1999). There was

## Clinical Vignette
### Engaging the Resistant Patient

Patient is brought in by parents and doesn't want to eat.

Patient:     You are not going to make me eat. I'm already too fat.

Therapist:   Well let's look at what it is about eating that distresses you, and let's see if there is any positive aspect to eating.

Patient:     I am too fat, I don't need to eat. Eating just makes me fatter and makes me feel worse.

Therapist:   Let's talk about what happens to your body if you do and don't eat, according to the research that scientists have done on this.

(Therapists should not enter into arguments, which they will inevitably lose. This is an opportunity to talk about the physical and psychological effects of starvation and results of studies like that of Keys study (see Section 4.1.1), engage the patient in motivational interviewing, and construct a cost-benefit analysis of not eating.)

Therapist:   You may not agree, but I think there's a part of you, the "anorexic" part, which is dominating at the moment – but there is a part of you which wants to "break free." The anorexic part is very strong, and this is partly because some of the effects of anorexia and starvation causes people, even "normal" young men like in the Keys study, to binge or overeat, and that makes you even more scared of your eating and weight getting out of control. Starvation also slows your body down, that's why you feel sick even when eating what looks like a "normal" meal, your stomach is emptying more slowly and you feel full more easily. What we need to do is to try and help you link into the nonanorexic part of you – you can think very easily about what's good for you about anorexia – what would be good about NOT having anorexia?

Patient:     Hmm, well maybe....I duuno... Oh – I suppose could feel OK about going out with my friends and not be terrified they will order up pizza or something.

no significant difference between MET and CBT in achieving a clinically significant reduction in binge frequency in participants with BN after four weeks using CBT *versus* MET. (See Section 4.5 for a more detailed discussion of MET.)

## 4.2.7    Conclusion

In summary, psychological therapies are the mainstay of the treatment of eating disorders, and a large number of different methods have been used to treat ED patients. It is up to the individual clinician to adopt the strategies that best address the needs of each particular patient. The following are common errors that can occur in any of these treatment modalities. The clinician should be aware of these errors in order to avoid making them.

**Clinical Vignette**
**Common Errors to Avoid in ED Therapy**

1. Pretending to an underweight patient that only a small amount of weight needs to be gained – although it may seem like a good way to get the patient engaged in treatment, it inevitably backfires when the patient then refuses to gain any further weight, stating "You said that would be enough, so I won't gain any more."
2. Failing to weigh the patient or letting the patient self-report her weight. This does not mean having the patient strip to her underwear to be weighed, but rather that one makes sure that pockets are empty, the patient hasn't just drunk a lot of water to distort her weight, or that she isn't wearing multiple layers of clothes.
3. Neglecting to have a thorough physical examination and relevant blood and other tests performed on a patient who appears to be at a reasonable weight and denies feeling unwell and/or purging.
4. Letting patients blame the treatment when they don't change – the patient will try to claim the therapeutic modality is wrong for her, or the staff is hindering her, and she thus evades responsibility for her own behavior.
5. Treating the mother or other family members instead of the patient – letting family members co-opt the therapy, e.g., letting the mother demand that you focus on a particular behavior such as vomiting, rather than engaging the patient in therapeutic change.
6. Letting patients get away with not doing daily food monitoring or other homework tasks – if the therapist doesn't pay attention to these tasks, the patient won't value them. If the patient doesn't want to do the homework, it will be impossible to engage the patient in doing other therapeutic tasks.
7. Allowing patients to avoid certain foods in the name of eating "healthy" foods. Patients may try to argue that they are vegetarian and will avoid all meats, proteins, and fats in the name of this. It is important to determine whether the vegetarianism (or other food avoidance) predated the eating disorder. It is also important to insist that a wide variety of foods be eaten, particularly emphasizing that healthy doesn't necessarily mean low calorie.
8. Allowing therapy to continue when the patient is becoming physically compromised and needs inpatient care (and thereby colluding with the belief that therapy is progressing despite the patient's physical deterioration).
9. Accepting "insight" from the patient or agreement with the therapist as evidence of change. Patients may begin to agree with the therapist that they are underweight but may continue to resist actually gaining any weight.

Patients also insist that they like food and like to eat, but that it makes them uncomfortable to eat, or say that they don't have AN because they know that they are thin. These are merely attempts to avoid therapy or changing.

## 4.3    Efficacy and Prognosis

### 4.3.1    Methods of Systematic Review

A systematic review of psychotherapies for treatment of eating disorders (Hay, 2008) was conducted for RCTs with at least one year follow-up (or RCTs otherwise of interest or high quality) that evaluated psychotherapies in common current use for AN, BN, BED, and EDNOS according to DSM-IV (APA, 1994) criteria or its equivalent.

The psychotherapies included in this review were deemed to be in common and/or current use and each had an evidence base of at least one longitudinal RCT. The therapies included the following: cognitive behavioral treatment (CBT) and other psychological approaches with a behavioral component, interpersonal psychotherapy (IPT), family therapy, self-help approaches, and these therapies in combination with antidepressant therapy. Trials of therapies not in common current use for eating disorders were excluded. These included a range of therapies that were obscure (such as cognitive orientation therapy) or that had been found to be ineffective (such as exposure plus response prevention enhancement of CBT). Studies evaluating behavioral therapies designed to address weight loss in people with obesity as well as an eating disorder were not included, unless the aim of treatment specifically was to attenuate eating disorder symptoms.

**Therapies chosen for review are evidence-based**

Outcomes of longitudinal (at least one year) randomized controlled studies were evaluated, where reported, across medical (weight/body mass index), psychiatric outcome status (e.g., abstinence from bulimic behaviors/frequency of eating disorder symptoms) and quality of life and/or social function domains.

Twenty-five RCTs were identified for inclusion from a total pool of 79 trials. The most common reason for exclusion of an RCT was failure to have at least one year of follow-up. Of the included studies, there were eight trials of BN patients, the majority looking at CBT-BN, other CBT, and combinations. When compared with another therapy, in one trial CBT-BN was found to be superior to interpersonal psychotherapy at end of treatment, but not at follow-up. CBT has been found to be at least as effective as antidepressants, but it is likely to be more acceptable to patients as higher dropout rates have been found in participants randomized to the drug arm of trials (see also Bacaltchuk & Hay, 2005a, b). Guided self-help CBT was supported in one trial, and a second study found that CBT may be effectively provided in a group setting. CBT appears to be more effective than BT alone. The quality of trials in the present review was variable; only one had adequate allocation concealment, five had blind outcome assessors, and four used intention-to-treat analyses.

There were eleven trials of AN patients, and two of these were post-hospitalization trials after some weight restoration. Most trials were inconclusive, although cognitive orientation and routine care therapy performed poorly. Trials were also very small with only four having more than 50 participants; only three utilized blind outcome assessors, and only three had adequate allocation concealment, although most did use intention-to-treat analyses. The newer nonspecific clinical management (see Section 4.2.2) approach showed some promise, but most participants did poorly in this and other trials.

There were six trials of treatment for BED, EDNOS, or mixed diagnostic groups. Outcomes in these trials were relatively better although not consistently so. CBT is the most well-evaluated treatment for these disorders, although it has proven difficult to demonstrate that it is more effective than an alternative therapy, namely IPT. In one trial, exercise was found to enhance psychological approaches in those with comorbid obesity. Four trials used intention-to-treat analyses, one had adequate allocation concealment, and none had blinded outcome assessment.

**Evidence supports the use of CBT and IPT for BN**

The results of this systematic review are consistent with other identified systematic reviews and guidelines. There is a limited body of evidence to support CBT-BN for treatment of BN in adults plus evidence that IPT is equally effective in most studies. An even more limited body of evidence supports the use of family therapy for treatment of AN in adolescents and children. CBT combined with weight management strategies, particularly exercise in adults with BED and a weight disorder, and self-help (especially guided CBT self-help) in BN, BED, and EDNOS adults show promise. In most trials treatment effects in BN, EDNOS, and BED appear to be sustained or even increase over time.

It should be noted there are many unanswered questions and overall the numbers of longitudinal trials are very low and of variable quality, and frequently likely to have been underpowered, especially for AN. There is insufficient research comparing active treatments with no treatment or wait-list groups. There is room for improvement in all approaches, in particular many patients with AN have a poor outcome even with the "best" of treatments. It is not known which of a range of approaches in either individual or family therapy for AN is most efficacious. This is highlighted by the unexpected results of the McIntosh et al. (2005) trial. Attempts to enhance CBT-BN, particularly with IPT, appear promising but have yet to be proven.

**There is little evidence of effective treatment for AN**

Readers might question why is there is so little evidence, in particular for the treatment of AN, the "oldest" of the eating disorders and the one causing the most disability? There are several putative explanations, including reluctance of patients and health care providers to take the chance of randomization to a potentially less effective therapy where the illness is severe and risk may be high. AN is more common in children and adolescents and often RCTs are less common where dual consent issues are present. In addition, AN is less common than other eating disorders. However, the lack of treatment trials in AN remains problematic.

A leading authority (Fairburn, 2005) has suggested that, given the poor outcome of RCTs in AN to date, further RCTs should not be conducted without preliminary data to support them. In order to study the mechanism and the rate of change of eating disorder treatments, further studies should also attempt to assess outcome during treatment and at follow-up, in addition to at the beginning of treatment.

## 4.3.2     Predictors of Outcome

Consistent predictors of outcome have proved elusive. The National Institute for Clinical Excellence (NICE, 2004) systematic search found only four consistent pre-treatment predictors of poorer outcome for treatment of BN: features of borderline personality disorder, concurrent substance misuse, low motivation for change, and a history of obesity. In addition, early progress in therapy predicted a better outcome at one (Agras et al., 2000) and three years (Carter et al., 2002), and a recent study has found higher "weight suppression," i.e., the discrepancy between an individual's highest weight ever and his or her present weight, to be associated with a higher dropout rate and poorer symptomatic outcome in patients treated for BN with CBT (Butryn, Lowe, Safer, & Agras, 2006).

Surprisingly, given the known association between low self-esteem and increased risk for eating disorders, self-efficacy has not been documented to have a large effect on outcome when measured (e.g., Agras et al., 2000). However, improvement in self-efficacy is an important goal of recovery for many patients.

## 4.4     Combinations with Medication

Evidence for combining psychotherapies with antidepressants is mainly confined to studies of antidepressants and psychotherapies in BN. A systematic review (Bacaltchuk & Hay, 2005a, b) concluded that the addition of antidepressants enhanced efficacy but at the cost of more participants not completing therapy. Psychotherapy added to antidepressant treatment also enhanced treatment effects. Grilo, Masheb, and Wilson (2005) found CBT to be more efficacious than CBT combined with fluoxetine (60 mg/day) in treating BED, and fluoxetine alone was similar in efficacy to placebo.

> Research suggests that the addition of medication enhanced efficacy in BN but at the cost of fewer patients completing therapy

However, with regards to combinations of specific antidepressants with CBT-BN, findings have been inconclusive. RCTs have found no significant differences in remission rates or symptoms between CBT for BN (CBT-BN) plus tricyclic antidepressants or fluoxetine, and CBT-BN or either antidepressant alone (Hay & Bacaltchuk, 2006).

If medication must be used, the best evidence supports high dose (60 mg a day) use of fluoxetine in BN. Fluoxetine may have a role in relapse prevention for BN, but this is based on only one study of a year's duration with very high attrition rates in the first three months (43% for fluoxetine and 74% for placebo; Romano, Halmi, Sarkar, Koke, & Lee, 2002). Results for relapse prevention in AN have been mixed. Finally, low dose olanzapine (e.g., 2.5 mg daily) may have a role in ameliorating behavioral agitation and ruminative thoughts in AN (Mondraty et al., 2005), but more studies are needed. It should always be remembered that patients with AN may have ECG changes (prolonged QTc intervals), which also occur with tricyclic antidepressants and some antipsychotics. Clinicians should use these medications with caution when treating AN.

> Fluoxetine may prevent replapses

## 4.5      Problems in Carrying out Treatment

When treating patients with eating disorders, and AN in particular, neither neophytes nor experienced clinicians will be able to escape the immutable fact that it will only be a matter of time before they will be confronted by a resistant or recalcitrant patient. The stakes become progressively higher when there is clear objective evidence that the patient is in a potentially life-threatening situation while nonetheless insisting that she has a right to determine her own destiny even if this results in her own demise. Nowhere in medicine do the forces of clinical imperativeness and the law collide so strongly as in the involuntary treatment of a patient with severe AN. It is difficult for both clinicians and society to decide if coercion should be part of accepted clinical practice or whether treatment should be a legal issue (Carney, Tait, Touyz, Ingvarson, Saunders, & Wakefield, 2006). Yet many clinicians working in the field of eating disorders would find it difficult to comprehend why there should be any consternation whatsoever about compulsory treatment in an illness that is a leading cause of death in young women. However, we are living in a changing world in which civil libertarians insist upon the importance of a balance between legislation that permits compulsory treatment and concerns about personal liberties. A further complexity is that there are differing sources of legal authority, including mental health and adult guardianship laws as well as common law. In a country such as the United States, which has a federal system of government, there are often different laws across states.

Rieger, Touyz, and Beumont (2002) recently reported that approximately 80% of patients with AN, who were inpatients in a specialist eating disorders unit were not actively engaged in treatment according to the Anorexia Nervosa Stages of Change Questionnaire (ANSOCQ). What was even more troubling was that the majority (i.e., 66%) of consenting patients were still not motivated to actively engage in treatment after an average length of admission of nearly three months. Despite the success of CBT in the treatment of patients with BN, its apparent failure in many patients with AN can be attributed in part to the ego-syntonic (highly valued) nature of the patient's symptoms. Anorexia nervosa patients resist embarking on a treatment designed to challenge their cognitions or to develop behavioral skills to resolve their symptoms (Dean, Touyz, Rieger, & Thornton, 2006). They often believe that such relinquishment of their absolute control over weight and food would result in an unacceptable threat to the fragile grasp with which they maintain their sense of identity and self-esteem (Goldner, 1989).

So how does a clinician engage a treatment-resistant patient with AN in therapy? Researchers have turned their attention to other disorders such as substance abuse, where there are also significant motivational deficits and where approaches such as motivational interviewing (MI) have shown promise (Cockell et al., 2002; Miller & Rollnick, 2002). The basic premise of MI is that motivation cannot be imposed by the clinician but rather rests within the individual patient, who can be encouraged to make use of it by means of a collaborative and empathic approach to treatment. This had led to the development of motivational enhancement therapy (MET), which requires the clinician to assist the patients to attain their own "change focused" objectives.

Some of the MET strategies that have been successfully implemented in an inpatient setting are documented below.

---

**Clinical Pearl**
**MET Strategies Employed in an Inpatient Setting**

---

*Note:* Most of these strategies are equally effective in the outpatient setting

- Educating patients about the transtheoretical model of change (DiClemente and Prochaska, 1998) that describes how patients can modify their aberrant behavior both within and outside formal treatment.
- Listing the benefits and costs of pursuing an eating disorder versus relinquishing it. The essential aim here is to get the patient to accept that the disadvantages of maintaining the disorder clearly surpass any perceived advantages (e.g., being unable to attend university or socialize with friends).
- Fostering an awareness of the incompatibility of entrenched eating disordered behaviors and the patients' ultimate life goals (see Feld, Woodside, Kaplan, Olmsted, & Carter, 2001, for a detailed description of this valuable technique). Patients are also encouraged to write a letter to the eating disorder as a "friend" and a follow-up letter to the disorder as an "enemy" (Schmidt & Treasure, 1997). This exercise has the dual purpose of further heightening the patient's awareness of the benefits and costs of maintaining the eating disorder, as well as externalizing it (i.e., separating the disorder from oneself).
- Exploring the origins of the eating disorder and its likely future role in the patient's life so as to exemplify the burdens, rather than the benefits, that are likely to ensue, i.e., what the eating disorder has stolen from her life (see Farrell, 2001, for a description of this technique which includes a visualization task in which patients are guided to imagine their life one year hence).
- Examining the advantages and disadvantages of recovery with an emphasis on the practical gains and losses for oneself as well as others (see Schmidt & Treasure, 1993, for a more detailed account). Patients are also asked for their view point regarding the following question: "If you were on your deathbed thinking about your life, what experiences do you think would stick out as most meaningful to you? Is your eating disorder involved in these experiences?" This exercise has the explicit purpose of encouraging patients to construe their lives as a whole, rather than through the distorted lens of the eating disorder.

Adapted from Dean et al., 2006.

---

These techniques are in addition to the basic principles of MI, which have been described by Miller and Rollnick (2002). The underlying and most important premise that characterizes this collaborative approach in therapy is the desire of the clinician to *elicit* motivation from the patient rather than *instill* it in her. This is ultimately achieved through:

- Conveying empathy and acceptance through the proficient use of reflective listening; e.g.,

    Patient:    But I just can't be 110 pounds – that's enormous!

    Therapist:    Yes, I know that's how it seems to you right now, that's because the anorexia seriously affects how you think about yourself and you weight, and I know it's really scary for you. What say, lets not talk about pounds anymore, lets just talk about being "healthy" – even thought I know having said that you'll now think when I say "healthy" I mean fat?

- Avoiding disputation by reframing the patient's arguments in a more positive direction (i.e., "rolling with resistance"). Patience is a distinct virtue with the oppositional patient.
- Validating the patient's self-efficacy; e.g.,

Patient:     I know I was never "good enough" for my Mum and Dad, even when I topped the class at school they pointed out I did it on an A– average.

Therapist:  Hmm... That sounds a pretty good results to me – was it you or your parents who minded most about the A– not being an A or A+. What did your teachers say?

Patient:     Oh, well I guess it was me as well. Teachers? Oh, they're always saying nice things – its just I'm never sure when to believe them...

Therapist:  What's important is what you believe about yourself. Let's look at some positives – can you tell me, maybe not right now but think about it over the next week..., what are some things you like a lot about yourself?

Armed with these techniques and strategies, the clinician is better able to form a relationship and assist the oppositional patients to overcome the impasse they find themselves in. This is intended to enable them to embark more successfully on the remainder of their treatment. The challenge for the clinician here is to "roll with the resistance" and avoid the common pitfall of becoming embroiled in a confrontational stand-off from which neither the clinician nor the patient gains.

---

**Clinical Pearl**
**Patience Is a Distinct Virtue with the Oppositional Patient**

---

"Rolling with resistance" and reframing the patient's statements in a more positive direction of change is the golden key to overcoming the impasses in treatment that so often occur. Like leaving a good red wine maturing in the cellar, the art of therapy is evident in not rushing in and directing the patient, although it is often tempting to do so. The rewards are much greater when the therapist ultimately guides oppositional patients to mobilize their own motivation to change and allows them to proceed towards recovery.

## 4.6    Compulsory Treatment

Unfortunately, despite their best efforts, clinicians may still find themselves with an intransigent patient in a life-threatening situation.

There may be little option but to contemplate compulsory treatment or guardianship. Griffiths, Beumont, Russell, Touyz, & Moore (1997) have formulated the following essential guidelines to make this somewhat foreboding task more palatable, especially for the less-experienced clinician.

*When to make the decision to embark on compulsory treatment*

- The decision to embark upon the involuntary treatment of an AN patient should only be made once due diligence has been given to the risks and perceived benefits to the patient.

- Consultation with all significant stakeholders should take place, including the patient, the patient's family, and the entire treatment team. Those involved should be provided with support, and recognition must be given to divergent viewpoints before, during, and after implementation. If this does not transpire, then these differences of opinion often produce a conflicted state of affairs where the fragile therapeutic alliance may be severely undermined. The golden rule here is painstaking consultation.
- The family has the right to know, and should be fully notified as to the reasons why treatment has been implemented against the patient's will, including the nature of the illness, the purported risks of not intervening, as well as the proposed treatment.

Where guardianship legislation exists, a parent may elect to act as the patient's guardian. However, this can be fraught with difficulty (and contraindicated) when the patient has a history of manipulating her parents. If this is the case, it is much more prudent to have a public guardian appointed.

As there are several different parties involved in involuntary treatment, it is absolutely essential that both a good rapport and open channel of communication are established between the treatment team, the guardian, and the immediate family. This becomes an even greater imperative when restrictive measures (such as parenteral or enteral nutrition) are indicated. It is usually invaluable to enlist the support of all parties concerned by discussing the lack of alternative options in what is often a somewhat desperate situation.

It is a long journey to recovery, and any given episode of involuntary treatment could be merely one of several episodes. In the end, successful cooperation by all concerned will be one of the essential components necessary to resolve the impasse. It is therefore especially important to address fears, anxieties, and guilt, not only just prior to the implementation of treatment, but throughout.

---

**Clinical Pearl**
**Being Decisive When the Situation Demands It**

When confronted by an angry, intransigent patient who is begging, pleading, and sobbing to be given yet another chance, with iron-clad guarantees of change and promises to do all that is asked, it is worth remembering some words of wisdom from experienced therapists. Most recovered patients who go on to survive their illness are deeply grateful that their clinician had the fortitude to withstand their relentless objections and pleas and acted decisively when the situation required it ("I wanted you to take control of the situation but couldn't get myself to ask you. I am so grateful that you did. You saved my life. Thank you!"). The motto here is "short-term pain for long-term gain."

---

## 4.7    Multicultural Issues

Studies of ethnic influences on eating disorders have mostly been confined to epidemiologic surveys in which "Western" groups are more likely to be surveyed. Immigration and acculturation stress appear to be important in increasing the risk of an eating disorder in women (see Hoek et al., 2003, for a full review and Section 3.4.3 above). While risk factors, severity, and phenomenology of eating disorders across cultures are most often more alike than different, and the needs for treatment similar, there is some evidence that presenting issues may differ across ethnic groups; for example, Black women with eating disorders may be less concerned about body size and shape than are White women (White, Kohlmaier, Varnado-Sullivan, & Williamson, 2003), may be less likely to access and/or receive psychotherapy (Striegel-Moore et al., 2005), with an increased likelihood of BED and nonpurging syndromes, and associated weight disorders (e.g., Striegel-Moore et al., 2005) and less likelihood of AN or BN (Striegel-Moore et al., 2003). Asian women may be more likely to under-report symptoms and/or not identify fat phobia (Lee & Lock, 2007).

**Although presentation of EDs may differ across ethnic groups, treatment is similar**

The *principles* of treatment of eating disorders are the same for patients of differing ethnic and cultural backgrounds. As with all psychological disorders, some aspects of therapy may differ because of variable cultural practices and social structures and therapy my need to be refocused accordingly. For example, inclusion of the grandparents may occur where patients come from ethnic groups where grandparents tend to be living in the family home. Therapist should be open to the possibility of an eating disorder and competent to offer therapy to patients from all ethnic groups.

An example of a modification of family therapy in AN is provided by Ma, Chow, Lee, and Lai (2002). They studies themes of the meaning of self-starvation in families received structural family therapy according to the Maudsley model in Hong Kong. Most themes were in consistent with those identified in "Western" studies with the additional theme of powerlessness and helplessness of the patient's mother. This powerlessness they argued reflected the conflicts experienced by Hong Kong women who are expected to be subservient to their husbands, while coping with the modernization of Hong Kong society. The authors described how they augmented the Maudsley model to incorporate such culturally specific themes.

# 5

# Case Vignettes

## Case Vignette 1: Tracey (Anorexia Nervosa)

Tracey was reluctantly taken to her family physician by her distraught parents after her mother unexpectedly walked into her bedroom. Tracey was about to get dressed after taking a shower, and this was the very first time that her mother had noticed the extent of her malnutrition. At that critical moment everything fell into place.

Tracey's mother was initially totally overcome by the shock of seeing her beautiful daughter's skeletal body, with protruding bones that were not unlike those seen in concentration camp survivors. Tracey lambasted her mother for walking into her room unannounced and vehemently denied the extent of her weight loss. Tracey showed her mother several magazines she had purchased arguing that she looked no different from many of the successful photographic models. Tracey's mother insisted on taking her straight to the medical center when she acknowledged that she had not had a menstrual period for several months. Tracey refused to go. Her mother then called her father who rushed home from work to persuade his daughter to seek medical assistance. Tracey remained absolutely defiant, insisting that both her parents were grossly overreacting. Her parents refused to let the matter rest and the arguments became more heated as time progressed, later involving both her younger brother and sister who insisted Tracey looked like she had anorexia. Despite the distress and concern expressed by the entire family, Tracey stood her ground and later locked herself into her room. After much negotiation, she agreed to join her family for dinner if they agreed not to take her to the medical center. Her mother thought she should at least be given a chance to eat a meal, whereas her father felt they were giving into her demands. This led to a further argument between her parents with her father accusing his wife of colluding with their daughter. As so often happens in cases like this, the parents became split in their decision-making; the patient then manipulated a compromise to her own advantage.

As her parents calmed down, they began to make sense of Tracey's aberrant behavior of the past six months. They had struggled to understand her odd behavior, but had eventually accepted it as part of adolescence. They simply had not seen through the smokescreen that Tracey had created in order to surreptitiously continue with her rigid weight-losing behaviors. She had persuaded her parents to allow her to go to school by bus with some of her friends, despite her mother having to take her younger siblings to the same school. This allowed Tracey to get off the bus several stops from school and from home so that she could walk the intervening distance. Tracey always seemed to be studying at

*Patient denies illness*

*Patient refuses treatment*

*Patient hides illness successfully until suddenly parents recognize the emaciation*

**Patient refuses to eat**

her friends' homes at dinner time telling her parents she was eating there. In fact, Tracey would tell her friends' parents that her mother would keep her dinner for her at home to heat up in the microwave when she returned. Tracey was becoming increasingly isolated, making all sorts of excuses as to why she couldn't go out. This was so she could deliberately avoid having to eat. Her parents eventually realized that their happy, extraverted, and popular adolescent daughter had become a recluse.

**Patient wears layers of clothes to stay warm**

Now they understood why she insisted on wearing baggy clothing, saying it was the current fashion trend. This allowed her to conceal the extent of her weight loss from the family. Also, she was always cold and "needed" extra layers of clothing to keep her warm.

**Patient was perfectionistic**

Tracey was consistently judged to be the most exceptional student in her class. She was both beautiful and academically gifted. She was also a superb cellist, and was the youngest member of the symphony orchestra ever to play the cello at an invited guest appearance. Tracey felt that if something was worth doing, it should be done well – in fact, perfectly. As far as her parents and peers were concerned, Tracey had it all. She had no equal. She had a loving, caring family, a father who was extremely successful at business and had accumulated significant wealth, and a mother who had become one of the first female barristers in their town. They lived in a beautiful home in the nicest part of town, and would regularly go away on exotic holidays. Tracey always wore the latest fashion designer clothes and had every conceivable material possession including an iPod, a new mobile phone, and one of the most expensive laptop computers money could buy. How could someone with so much end up in the situation that Tracey found herself in?

Tracey's weight loss had in fact commenced after the boy she was particularly keen on invited one of her friends to his formal instead of her. Tracey found this almost impossible to comprehend, and when one of his friends told her that he liked her friend's cute bum, she decided she needed to lose weight. Tracey made a promise to herself that no one else would ever be thinner than her, that she would never be rejected because of her appearance. Thus began a journey of deliberate starvation.

**Patient takes control of cooking/food preparation**

Tracey did keep her side of the bargain and joined the family for dinner. Her parents breathed a sigh of relief. However, this was very short-lived. Tracey immediately accused her mother of deliberately pouring oil all over the food and refused to eat any of it. Her mother then reluctantly agreed to make her a meal which she could observe so she could see no oil being used in its preparation. But when it came to eating it, Tracey insisted that her mother had filled her plate to excess and she wouldn't be able to eat all of the food.

**Patient eats in ritualized manner, cutting up food into small pieces, moving it around on the plate, but not eating much**

Tracey then began to play with her food, dissecting the quiche into small parts and pushing it around her plate. Her father eventually lost his patience and tried to grab her arm to push the food into her mouth. Tracey jumped up from the table and ran out of the house into the street. Tracey's mother then blamed her father for causing Tracey to miss her meal. Both her younger siblings burst into tears as her father ran after Tracey saying she was going to die. Tracey was eventually persuaded to return home on the condition that she would see a doctor. However, she made her parents promise her that if her doctor agreed with her that her parents were overreacting, they would leave her alone. Although they were aware that they were being manipulated by Tracey, they felt they would do whatever it took to get her to the medical centre.

It did not take their family physician much time to diagnose Tracey with anorexia nervosa. Her behaviors were the classical ones seen in this disorder, and her deceit was transparent. The precipitating factor was not an uncommon one. The family physician insisted that Tracey be assessed for admission at the local eating disorder unit affiliated with the university teaching hospital. Tracey insisted that if they followed through with this, she would run away and kill herself. This frightened her parents who pleaded with the physician for Tracey to be given another chance. Tracey was promising to eat whatever the doctor or dietitian would prescribe for her. She insisted that she had learned her lesson, realized that she needed to gain weight, and would do exactly as she was told. With much trepidation and against their doctor's advice, they took her home, with her mother deciding to take a month off work to supervise her eating. However by lunch the following day, Tracey admitted she was unable to eat her meal and reluctantly agreed to an assessment at the eating disorder unit.

**Patient resorts to threats of self-harm to avoid treatment**

**Patient is finally convinced to accept treatment, when forced to see she cannot change on her own**

## Case Vignette 2: Belinda (Bulima Nervosa)

Belinda is a 23-year-old receptionist engaged to be married in six months. Her fiancé is a successful young lawyer. They have known each other for three years.

Belinda is the youngest of three children. She has two older brothers, both of whom have been described as having "large frames." Belinda's father is obese and her mother has dieted as long as she can remember. However, despite this, she has never been satisfied with her weight and constantly desires to be thinner.

**Patient's family has history of overweight**

Belinda was a pudgy child and her mother tried to keep sweets and cakes away from her. When she became an adolescent, her mother became more vocal in her concerns about Belinda's weight, telling her she would never have a boyfriend unless she lost weight. Eventually her mother persuaded her to attend a commercial weight-loss program and, much to everyone's delight, Belinda lost 12 kg. However, no sooner had she discontinued the program, when she began to regain the weight she had lost. She significantly increased her level of activity, attending the gym six days per week for an hour each time engaging in vigorous aerobic exercise. Belinda also started to walk as much as she could.

**Patient starts formal dieting and loses some weight, but regains it**

When she was 17 her first relationship ended so she decided to go on a strict diet. Over the next three months she lost 12 kg, giving her a Body Mass Index of 23. Her self-esteem improved dramatically. She became even more determined to lose further weight and decided to restrict herself to one small salad each evening and to drink as much water as she could during the day to feel satiated.

**Patient restricts her eating drastically despite weight in normal range**

All of this came to an end during her last year of high school. Belinda had hoped to gain a high enough mark to attend a university, despite her teachers saying this was unlikely because of a long-standing learning disability. When she received the results of one of her examinations in which she did poorly, Belinda became distressed and tearful at home. She noticed that her mother bought a birthday cake for her brother's birthday. She couldn't resist picking at the cake just to taste it. However, once she did this, she felt compelled just to have a little bit more and after an hour had eaten the entire cake. Belinda felt physically ill, bloated, and disgusted by her behavior. She went to the bathroom and while there felt some of the cake regurgitating into her mouth. The thought entered her mind that if she actually vomited, she might feel better, and she did so. However, she wasn't sure that she had "vomited up" the entire cake and became fearful that she would gain weight as a result of it. She then walked to the pharmacy and bought both ipecac and laxatives. She used the ipecac to induce vomiting a second time, unaware of the serious medical danger she risked in doing so. To ensure that she would be left with absolutely no cake in her digestive system, she swallowed the entire contents of the packet of laxatives. She replaced the cake she had eaten telling her mother that she had accidentally knocked it onto the floor. Belinda felt guilty about lying to her mother.

Belinda found it increasingly difficult to keep to her rigid and restrictive food plan. Whenever she deviated one iota from it (which was becoming increasing common), she would make herself vomit. Once having made the decision to vomit, Belinda felt the need to avail herself of what she considered to be the last opportunity to indulge herself in her favorite foods that she would never ever eat again. And so she would gorge herself as if this was the last time. Her bingeing was always done in secret at home when everyone was out of the house. Because of the embarrassing saga with her brother's birthday cake, Belinda would deliberately go to several supermarkets (to avoid the embarrassment of buying so many energy dense foods) to buy the food she would later binge on. She did not want her mother to notice that any food was missing from the pantry. Because of all the food she was purchasing, she was becoming indebted to all around her.

After she completed high school and during her first year of secretarial college, Belinda vomited blood. This terrified her, and she immediately consulted her general practitioner. After conducting the appropriate blood tests and an ECG, which were all normal, he referred her to a clinical psychologist and prescribed 60 mg of Prozac (fluoxetine) per day. The clinical psychologist blamed the eating disorder on her mother's obsession with weight and shape, and wanted to explore their relationship in greater depth. Belinda liked the clinical psychologist and attended for six sessions, but because there was no change in her bingeing or vomiting, she discontinued these sessions. She kept trying to diet but the more she tried to do so, the more she seemed to binge. Belinda became increasing moody and tearful and on a Sunday evening, after bingeing and vomiting throughout the day, she confronted her boyfriend saying that he was more interested in his new attractive work partner than in her because the other girl was thinner. She insisted that he would leave her despite his assertions to the contrary. She felt unable to let the matter rest and the arguments escalated until he walked out of the house. Belinda became increasing distressed, and her parents were unable to console her. She was unable to sleep and at 6 am sent her boyfriend a text message on his phone. When he failed to reply after 5 minutes, she overdosed on her SSRI, hoping to use sleep to escape her pain. Her mother was unable to wake her up at midday and phoned for an ambulance.

**Patient is upset with herself for bingeing and vomits to get rid of food (first time may or may not be intentional)**

**Patient escalates purging efforts by taking laxatives and/or diuretics**

**Bingeing and vomiting are done in secret**

**Patient tries therapy but if bingeing is not addressed, patient gives up**

**Patient attempts suicide or other self-harm (impulse control problem)**

# Case Vignette 3: Mark (Binge Eating Disorder)

Mark is a 37-year-old white, single male. He is an accountant for a large firm. Ever since he was a child he recalls haven been larger and having a larger appetite than his friends. His mother encouraged him to eat: "Mark is a growing boy. He needs his food." When he was in grade school he enjoyed playing sports, but when he went to high school, because of his increasing weight, he was too embarrassed to try to play any sport and he began to spend almost all of his free time playing videogames on his computer.

*Patients have a history of overweight or obesity*

Throughout his high school years his weight increased, and he had very few dates. Although he was interested in girls, he was shy and felt too self-conscious about his size to ask them out. He recalls being quite lonely at university, avoiding those social settings where he would feel embarrassed. Instead he ate alone to comfort himself.

*Patients are often socially isolated, and use food to self-medicate mood*

When he graduated from college and began work, the company required he have a medical assessment for insurance purposes. Although he wasn't obese, his weight was high enough that the doctor felt he would benefit from losing 25–30 pounds.

He tried dieting, and he was initially successful. Mark lost 80 pounds in less than 6 months, but soon found himself craving his favorite food. He started cheating on his diet, felt guilty for cheating and decided he would enjoy himself today and start dieting tomorrow. This soon escalated into eating binges where he felt out of control and ate until he was physically uncomfortable and exhausted.

*BED patients may diet to compensate for bingeing, but often the binges follow diet attempts*

This became a pattern. Mark would try to diet, but something would happen and he would break his diet and binge for the rest of the day, always promising himself that he would go back on his diet the next day. He felt too uncomfortable to exercise and never tried anything else to compensate for his overeating. So his weight gradually increased further. He tried some commercial diet programs and even a diet book, but none of these seemed to help.

As his weight escalated, Mark became dysphoric. The only people he socialized with were his brother, who was also overweight, and one heavy friend from work.

In the context of his increasing isolation, dysphoric mood, and ever-increasing weight, Mark decided he needed to lose weight at all cost. He consulted a nutritionist, who prescribed a strict diet with exercise, which he was only able to follow for a couple of weeks. He felt so guilty that he wasn't keeping to his meal plan and not exercising, that he cancelled his appointments with the nutritionist. He finally got so desperate that he consulted a doctor to ask for a referral for treatment for his problem.

*Patients give up on treatments that don't seem to be helping*

# 6

# Further Reading

Birmingham, C. L., & Beumont, P. (2004). *Medical management of eating disorders*. Cambridge, UK: Cambridge University Press.

This is an excellent resource book illustrating the medical management of patients with eating disorders. It has a practical focus and is essential for those practitioners who need to familiarize themselves with medical issues and their management. This book is easy to read and those without medical training will find it invaluable.

Bruch, H. (1978). *The golden cage: The enigma of anorexia nervosa*. Cambridge, MA: Harvard University Press.

Hilde Bruch was the first to depict anorexia nervosa from the patient's perspective, and to understand the pressures to succeed that seem to underlie the disorder. At the time this book was written, Western women were breaking out of the societal cages that constrained them, but for some, this freedom was too threatening, so they created their own cages. This is an excellent book for patients, parents, physicians, and anyone who might come into contact with a potential anorexic patient during the early stages of the pathology.

Fairburn, C. (1995). *Overcoming binge eating*. New York: Guilford.

This is essentially a self-help text with a very strong practical emphasis. It is based upon evidence-based research undertaken by the Oxford group, and the book provides good practical skills for patients to learn. Many clinicians use this book as an adjunct to treatment.

Garner, D. M., & Garfinkel, P. E. (Eds.) (1997). *Handbook of psychotherapy of eating disorders* (2nd edition). New York: Guilford.

Although a little dated, this remains the most comprehensive handbook for the treatment of eating disorders. It is especially helpful to those clinicians who have not had much training in eating disorders. This book covers most of the therapies commonly used in eating disorders and has a practical focus.

Grilo, C. M. (2006). *Eating and weight disorders*. Hove, UK: Psychology Press.

This recently published book provides a comprehensive review of the field focusing on all the major eating disorders including AN, BN, atypical eating disorders, and BED as well as obesity. This is an excellent resource book, which incorporates the most up to date research and provides an authoritative overview of the state of the art in eating disorders. It is an ideal text for those who are not specialists in the field.

Lock, J., & le Grange, D. (2005). *Help your teenager beat an eating disorder*. New York: Guilford.

This book, written by two leading experts in the field, provides good practical advice on how to treat teenagers with eating disorders. As many patients presenting with eating disorders are adolescents, this book provides valuable advice about how best to treat this group of patients.

National Institute for Health and Clinical Excellence (2004). *Eating disorders – Core interventions in the treatment management of anorexia nervosa, bulimia nervosa, and related eating disorders*. London: Author. Available at http://guidance.nice.org.uk/CG9.

The NICE guidelines are an encyclopedia of knowledge regarding a consensus-based approach to the treatment of eating disorders. The clinician is quickly able to ascertain which evidence-based treatments are recommended and where they can be found.

Schmidt, U., & Treasure, J. (1993). *Getting better bit(e) by bit(e)*. Hove, UK: Psychology Press.

This is an excellent text that vividly portrays the specific problems faced by patients with bulimia nervosa. It is easy to read, illustrated with real-life vignettes and is based on proven clinical trials. This self-help text provides many practical strategies that the less-experienced therapist will find very useful.

Waller, G., Cordery, H., Corstorphine, E., Hinrichsen, H., Lawson, R., Mountford, V., Russell, K. (2007). *Cognitive Behavioral Therapy for Eating Disorders: A Comprehensive Treatment Guide*. Cambridge, UK: Cambridge University Press.

This recently published book is an excellent resource for learning innovative cognitive-behavioral strategies to implement with patients with eating disorders. This book is well suited to both the generalist therapist as well as for those who have specialized in the treatment of eating disorders.

# 7

# References

Abed, R. T. (1998). The sexual competition hypothesis for eating disorders. *British Journal of Medical Psychology*, *71*, 525–547.

Adkins, E. D., & Peel, P. K. (2005). Does excessive or compulsive best describe exercise as a symptom of bulimia nervosa? *International Journal of Eating Disorders*, *38*, 24–29.

Agras, W. S, Crow, S., Halmi, K., Mitchell, J. E., Wilson, G. T., & Kraemer, H. C. (2000). Outcome predictors for the cognitive-behavior treatment of bulimia nervosa: Data from a multisite study. *American Journal Psychiatry*, *157*, 1302–1308.

Agras, W. S., Schneider, J. A., Arnow, B., Raeburn, S. D., & Telch, C. F. (1989). Cognitive-behavioral and response-prevention treatments for bulimia nervosa. *Journal of Consulting and Clinical Psychology, 57*, 215–221.

American Psychiatric Association (1987). *Diagnostic and statistical manual of mental disorders* (3rd ed., rev.). Washington, DC: American Psychiatric Association.

American Psychiatric Association (1994). *Diagnostic and statistical manual of mental disorders* (4th ed.). Washington, DC: American Psychiatric Association.

American Psychiatric Association (2000a). *Diagnostic and statistical manual of mental disorders* (4th ed., text revision) Washington, DC: American Psychiatric Association.

American Psychiatric Association (2000b). Practice guidelines for the treatment of patients with eating disorders (revision). *American Journal Psychiatry*, *157 Suppl*ement, 1–39.

Bacaltchuk, J., & Hay, P. (2005a). Antidepressants versus placebo for people with bulimia nervosa. *Cochrane Database of Systematic Reviews, 4,* Art. No.: CD003391.

Bacaltchuk, J., & Hay P. (2005b). Antidepressants versus psychological treatments and their combination for people with bulimia nervosa. *Cochrane Database of Systematic Reviews, 4,* Art. No.: CD003385.

Bachar, E., Yael, L., Shulamit, K., & Berry, E. M. (1999). Empirical comparison of two psychological therapies: Self Psychology and Cognitive Orientation in the Treatment of Anorexia and Bulimia. *Journal of Psychotherapy Practice and Research, 2,* 115–128.

Banasiak, S. J., Paxton, S. J., & Hay, P. J. (2007). Guide of self-help for bulimia nervosa in primary care: A randomized control trial. *Psychological Medicine, 3S,* 1283–1294.

Beck, A. T. (1976). *Cognitive therapy and the emotional disorders*. New York. International Universities Press.

Beck, A. T., Rush, A. J., Shaw, B. F., & Emery, G. (1979). Cognitive therapy of depression. New York: Guilford Press.

Bemis, K. (1987). The present status of operant conditioning for the treatment of anorexia nervosa. *Behavior Modification, 11*, 432–463.

Bemporad, J. R. (1997). Cultural and historical aspects of eating disorders. *Theoretical Medicine, 18*, 401–420.

Beumont, P. J. V. (2002). Clinical presentation of anorexia nervosa and bulimia nervosa. In C. G. Fairburn & K. D. Brownell (Eds.), *Eating disorders and obesity: A comprehensive handbook* (pp. 162–170). New York: The Guilford Press.

Beumont, P. J. V., Arthur, B., Russell, J. D., & Touyz, S. (1994). Excessive physical activity in dieting disorder patients: Proposals for a supervised exercise program. *International Journal of Eating Disorders*, *15*, 21–36.

Beumont, P. J. V., Beumont, C. C., Touyz, S. W., & Williams, H. (1997). Nutritional counseling and supervised exercise. In D. M. Garner & P. E. Garfinkel (Eds), *Handbook of treatment for eating disorders* (2nd ed., pp. 178–187). New York: The Guilford Press.

Beumont, P., Hay, P., Beumont, D., Birmingham, L., Derham, H., & Jordan, A., et al. (2004). Australian and New Zealand clinical practice guidelines for the treatment of anorexia nervosa. *Australian and New Zealand Journal of Psychiatry*, *38*, 659–670.

Beumont, P. J. V., & Touyz, S. W. (2003). What kind of illness is anorexia nervosa? *European Child and Adolescent Psychiatry*, *12*, Supplement 1, 20–24.

Birmingham, L., & Beumont, P. (2004). *Medical management of eating disorders*. Cambridge University Press, Cambridge.

Booth, D. A. (1988). Culturally corralled into food abuse: The eating disorders as physiologically reinforced excessive appetites. In K. M. Pirke, W. Vandereycken, & D. Ploog (Eds.), *The psychobiology of bulimia nervosa* (pp. 18–32). Berlin: Springer-Verlag.

Braun, D. L., Sunday, S. R., Huang, A., & Halmi, K. A. (1999). More males seek treatment for eating disorders. *International Journal of Eating Disorders*, *25*, 415–424.

Bruch, H. (1973). *Eating disorders*. New York: Basic Books, Inc.

Bruch, H. (1975). Obesity and anorexia nervosa: Psychosocial aspects. *Australia and New Zealand Journal of Psychiatry*, *9*, 159–161.

Bruch, H. (1978). *The golden cage: The enigma of anorexia nervosa*. Cambridge, MA: Harvard University Press.

Bryant-Waugh, R., Cooper, R., Taylor, C., & Lask, B. D. (1996). The use of the Eating Disorder Examination with children: A pilot study. *International Journal of Eating Disorders*, *19*, 391–397.

Bulik, C. M., Sullivan, P. F., Carter, F. A., & Joyce, P. R. (1997). Initial manifestations of disordered eating behavior: Dieting versus bingeing. *International Journal of Eating Disorders*, *22*, 195–201.

Butryn, M. L., Lowe, M. R., Safer, D. L., & Agras, W. S. (2006). Weight suppression is a robust predictor of outcome in the cognitive-behavioral treatment of bulimia nervosa. *Journal of Abnormal Psychology*, *115*, 62–67.

Byrne, S. M., & McLean, N. J. (2002). The cognitive-behavioral model of bulimia nervosa: A direct evaluation. *International Journal of Eating Disorders*, *31*, 17–31.

Carlat, D. J., & Carmago, C. A. (1991). Review of bulimia nervosa in males. *American Journal of Psychiatry*, *148*, 831–843.

Carney, T., Tait, D., Touyz, S., Ingvarson, M., Saunders, D., & Wakefield, A. (2006). *Managing anorexia nervosa: Clinical, legal, and social perspectives on involuntary treatment*. New York: Nova.

Carter, F. A., Bulik, C. M., McIntosh, V. V., & Joyce, P. (2002). Cue reactivity as a predictor of outcome with bulimia nervosa. *International Journal of Eating Disorders*, *31*, 240–250.

Cash, T. F. (1991). *Body image therapy: A program for self-directed change* (Audiocasette series including client workbook). New York: Guilford.

Cash, T. F. (1995). *What do you see when you look in the mirror? Helping yourself to a positive body image*. New York: Bantam Books.

Chen, E., Touyz, S. W., Beumont, P. J. V., Fairburn, C. G., Griffiths, R., Butow, P., et al. (2002). A comparison of group and individual cognitive-behavioral therapy for patients with bulimia nervosa. *International Journal of Eating Disorders*, *33*, 241–254.

Cockell, J., Geller, J., & Linden, W. (2002). The development of a decisional balance scale for anorexia nervosa. *European Eating Disorders Review*, *10*, 359–375.

Coelho, J., Thornton, C., Touyz, S., Lacey, J. H., & Corfe, S. (2007). Eating disorders and drug and alcohol problems. In A. Baker, & R. Velleman (Eds.), *Clinical handbook or co-existing mental health and drug and alcohol problems* (pp. 290–308). London: Brunner-Routledge.

Collier, D. A., & Treasure, J. L. (2004). The aetiology of eating disorders. *British Journal of Psychiatry*, *185*, 363–365.

Cooper, M. J. (2005). Cognitive theory in anorexia nervosa and bulimia nervosa: Progress, development, and future directions. *Clinical Psychology Review*, *25*, 511–531.

Cooper, P. (1995). *Bulimia nervosa and binge eating: A guide to recovery*. London: Robinson Press.

Cooper, P. J., Taylor, M. J., Cooper, Z., & Fairburn, C. G. (1987). The development and validation of the body shape questionnaire. *International Journal of Eating Disorders*, *6*, 485–494.

Cooper, Z., & Fairburn, C. G. (2003). Refining the definition of BED and non-purging bulimia nervosa. *International Journal of Eating Disorders*, *34*, S89–S95.

Crandall, C. (1988). Social contagion of binge eating. *Journal of Personality and Social Psychology*, *55*, 588–598.

Dare, C., & Crowther, J. C. (1995). Living dangerously: Psychoanalytic psychotherapy of anorexia nervosa. In G. Szmulker, C. Dare, & J. Treasure, (Eds.). *Handbook of Eating Disorders: Theory, treatment, and research* (pp.125–139). Chichester, UK: John Wiley & Sons.

Davis, C., & Claridge, G. (1998). The eating disorders as addiction: A psychobiological perspective. *Addictive Behaviors*, *23*, 463–475.

Davis, C., Katzman, D. K., & Kirsh, C. (1999). Compulsive physical activity in adolescents with anorexia nervosa – A psychobehavioral spiral of pathology. *Journal of Nervous and Mental Disease*, *187*, 336–342.

Davis, C., & Woodside, D. B. (2002). Sensitivity to the rewarding effects of food and exercise in the eating disorders. *Comprehensive Psychiatry*, *43*, 189–194.

Dean, H. Y., Touyz, S. W., Rieger, E., & Thornton, C. E. (2006). Can motivational enhancement therapy improve a cognitive behaviorally based inpatient program for eating disorders? In D. Einstein (Ed.), *Innovations and Advances in Cognitive Behavior Therapy*. Sydney: Australian Academic Press.

Delinsky, S. S., & Wilson, G. T. (2006). Mirror exposure for the treatment of body image disturbance. *International Journal of Eating Disorders*, *39*, 108–116.

DiClemente, C. C., & Prochaska, J. O. (1998). Toward a comprehensive, transtheoretical model of change. In W. R. Miller & N. Heather (Eds). *Treating addictive behaviors* (2nd ed.). New York: Plenum Press.

Dolan, B., & Gitzinger, I. (1994). Why women? *Gender issues and eating disorders*. London: The Athlone Press.

Fairburn, C. G. (1995). *Overcoming binge eating*. New York: Guilford Press.

Fairburn, C. G. (2002). Cognitive-behavioral therapy for bulimia nervosa. In C. G. Fairburn & K. D. Brownell (Eds.), *Eating disorders and obesity: A comprehensive handbook* (2nd edition, pp. 302–307). New York: Guilford.

Fairburn, C. G. (2005) Evidenced based treatment of anorexia nervosa. *International Journal of Eating Disorders*, *37*, S26–S30.

Fairburn, C. G. (in press). Transdiagnostic cognitive behavior therapy for eating disorders. New York: Guilford Press.

Fairburn C. G., & Bohn, K. (2005). Eating Disorder NOS (EDNOS): An example of the troublesome 'Not Otherwise Specified' (NOS) category in DSM-IV. *Behaviour Research and Therapy*, *43*, 691–701.

Fairburn, C. G., & Cooper, Z. (1993). The eating disorder examination (12th edition). In C. G. Fairburn & G. T. Wilson (Eds.), *Binge eating: Nature, assessment, and treatment* (pp.317–360). New York: Guilford Press.

Fairburn, C. G., Cooper, Z., Doll, H. A., Norman, P., & O'Connor, M. (2000). The natural course of bulimia nervosa and BED in young women. *Archives of General Psychiatry*, *57*, 659–665.

Fairburn, C. G., Cooper, Z., & Shafran, R. (2003). Cognitive behavior therapy for eating disorders: A "transdiagnostic" theory and treatment. *Behaviour Research and Therapy*, *41*, 509–529.

Fairburn, C. G., & Harrison, P. J. (2003). Eating disorders. *The Lancet*, *361*, 407–416.

Fairburn, C. G., Jones, R., Peveler, R., Carr, S. J., Solomon, R. A., O'Connor, M. E., Burton, J., & Hope, R. A. (1991). Three psychological treatments for bulimia nervosa: A comparative trial. *Archives of General Psychiatry*, *48*, 463–469.

Fairburn, C. G., Marcus, M. D., & Wilson, G. T. (1993). Cognitive behavior therapy for binge eating and bulimia nervosa: A comprehensive treatment manual. In C. G. Fairburn & G. T. Wilson, (Eds.), *Binge Eating: Nature, Assessment, and Treatment* (pp. 361–404). New York: The Guilford Press.

Fairburn, C. G., & Walsh, B. T. (2002). Atypical eating disorders (Eating disorder not otherwise specified). In C. G. Fairburn & K. D. Brownell (Eds.), *Eating disorders and obesity: A comprehensive handbook* (pp. 171–177). New York: The Guilford Press.

Fairburn, C. G., Welsh, S. L., Doll, H. A., Davies, B. A., & O'Connor, M. E. (1997). Risk factors for bulimia nervosa – A community-based case-control study. *Archives of General Psychiatry, 54*, 509–517.

Farrell, C. (2001). The use of motivational interviewing techniques in offending behavior group work. *Motivational Interviewing Newsletter, 8*, 8–12.

Farrell, C., Shafran, R., & Lee, M. (2006). Empirically evaluated treatments for body image disturbance: A review. *European Eating Disorders Review, 14*, 289–300.

Feld, R., Woodside, D. B., Kaplan, A. A., Olmsted, M. P., & Carter, J. (2001). Pretreatment motivational enhancement therapy for eating disorders: A pilot study. *International Journal of Eating Disorders, 29*, 393–400.

Fennell, M. (1999). *Overcoming low self-esteem*. Robinson: London.

First, M. B., Spitzer, R. L., Gibbon, M. A., & Williams, J. B. (1996). *Structured clinical interview for DSM-IV axis 1 disorders – Non-patient edition*. New York: New York State Psychiatric Institute.

Garfinkel, P. E. (2002). Classification and diagnosis of eating disorders. In C. G. Fairburn & K. D. Brownell (Eds.), *Eating disorders and obesity: A comprehensive handbook* (pp. 155–161). New York: The Guilford Press.

Garner, D. M. (1991). *The eating disorder inventory*. Lutz, FL: Psychological Assessment Resources, Inc.

Garner, D. M., & Garfinkel P. E. (1997). *Handbook of treatment for eating disorders* (2nd ed.). New York: The Guilford Press.

Garner, D. M., & Needleman, L. D. (1997). Sequencing and integration of treatments. In D. M. Garner & P. E. Garfinkel (Eds.), *Handbook of treatment for eating disorders* (2nd ed., pp. 50–66). New York: The Guilford Press.

Garner, D. M., Olmsted, M. P., Bohr, Y., & Garfinkel, P. E. (1982). The eating attitudes test: Psychometric features and clinical correlates. *Psychological Medicine, 12*, 871–878.

Garner, D. M., Olmsted, M. P., & Polivy, J. (1983). Development and validation of a multi-dimensional eating disorder inventory for anorexia nervosa and bulimia. *International Journal of Eating Disorders, 2*, 15–34.

Garner, D. M., Olmsted, M. P., Polivy, J., & Garfinkel, P. E. (1984). Comparison between weight-preoccupied women and anorexia nervosa. *Psychosomatic Medicine, 46*, 255–266.

Garner, D. M., Vitousek, K. M., Pike, K. M. (1997). Cognitive-behavioral therapy for anorexia nervosa. In D. M. Garner & P. E. Garfinkel (Eds), *Handbook of treatments for eating disorders* (2nd ed., pp. 94–144). New York: The Guilford Press.

Geller, J., Johnston, C., & Madsen, K. (1997). The role of shape and weight in self-concept: The shape and weight-based self-esteem inventory. *Cognitive Therapy and Research, 21*, 5–24.

Gendall, K. A., Sullivan, P. F., Joyce, P. R., Fear, J. L., & Bulik, C. M. (1997). Psychopathology and personality of young women who experience food cravings. *Addictive Behaviors, 22*, 545–555.

Gleaves, D. H., Lowe, M. R., Snow, A. C., Green, B. A., & Murphy-Eberenz, K. P. (2000). Continuity and discontinuity models of bulimia nervosa: A taxometric investigation. *Journal of Abnormal Psychology, 109*, 56–68.

Goldner, E. (1989). Treatment refusal in anorexia nervosa. *International Journal of Eating Disorders, 8*, 297–306.

Goodsitt, A. (1997). Eating disorders: A self-psychological perspective. In D. M. Garner & P. E. Garfinkel, (Eds), *Handbook of treatments for eating disorders* (2nd ed., pp. 205–228). New York: The Guilford Press.

Green, M. W., Elliman, N. A., Wakeling, A., & Rogers, P. J. (1996). Cognitive functioning, weight change and therapy in anorexia nervosa. *Journal of Psychiatric Research, 30*, 401–410.

Griffiths, R. A., Beumont, P. J. V., Russell, J., Touyz, S. W., & Moore, G. (1997). The use of guardianship legislation for anorexia nervosa: A report of 15 cases. *Australian and New Zealand Journal of Psychiatry*, *31*, 525–531.

Griffiths, R. A., Hadzi-Pavlovic, D., & Channon-Little, L. (1996). The short-term follow-up effect of hypnobehavioral and cognitive behavioral treatment for bulimia nervosa. *European Eating Disorders Review*, *4*, 12–31.

Grilo, C. M. (2006). *Eating and weight disorders*. New York: Psychology Press.

Grilo, C. M., & Masheb, R. M. (2002). Childhood maltreatment and personality disorders in adult patients with binge eating disorder. *Acta Psychiatrica Scandinavica*, *106*, 183–188.

Grilo, C. M., Masheb, R. M., & Wilson, G. T. (2005). Efficacy of cognitive behavioral therapy and fluoxetine for the treatment of binge eating disorder: A randomized double-blind placebo-controlled comparison. *Biological Psychiatry*, *57*, 301–309.

Grilo, C. M., Sanislow, C. A., Shea, M. T., Skodol, A. E., Stout, R. L., Pagano, M. E., et al. (2003). The natural course of bulimia nervosa and eating disorder not otherwise specified is not influenced by personality disorders. *International Journal of Eating Disorders*, *34*, 319–330.

Hay, P. (2008). Eating disorders. In J. A. Trafton & W. Gordon, (Eds.), *Best practices in the behavioral management of health from preconception to adolescence*. Los Altos, CA: The Institute for Brain Potential.

Hay, P. J., & Bacaltchuk, J. (2006). Bulimia nervosa. *Clinical Evidence*, *15*, 1315–1331.

Hay, P. J., Bacaltchuk, J., & Stefano, S. (2004). Psychotherapy for bulimia nervosa and binge eating. *Cochrane Database of Systematic Reviews, 3*, CD000562.

Hay, P. J., & Fairburn, C. G. (1998). The validity of the DSM-IV scheme for classifying bulimic eating disorders. *International Journal of Eating Disorders*, *23*, 7–15.

Hay, P., & Touyz, S. (2007). Eating disorders. In S. Bloch & B. S. Singh (Eds.), *Foundations of clinical psychiatry* (pp. 235–250). Melbourne University Press, Melbourne.

Heatherton, T. F., & Polivy, J. (1992). Chronic dieting and eating disorders: A spiral model. In J. H. Crowther, S. E. Hobfall, M. A. P. Stephens, & D. L. Tennenbaum (Eds.), *The etiology of bulimia: The individual and familial context* (pp. 133–155). Washington, DC: Hemisphere Publishers.

Hill, S., & Touyz, S. W. (2007). Maladaptive schemas and eating disorders: Therapeutic considerations. In D. A. Einstein (Ed.), *Innovations and advances in cognitive behavior therapy*. Bowen Hills, Australia: Australia Academic Press.

Hoek, H. W. (2002). Distribution of eating disorders. In C. G. Fairburn & K. D. Brownell (Eds.), *Eating disorders and obesity: A comprehensive handbook* (pp. 233–237). New York: The Guilford Press.

Hoek, H. W., van Hoeken, D., & Katzman, M.. (2003). Epidemiology and cultural aspects of eating disorders: A review. In M. Maj & K. Halmi (Eds). *Eating disorders: Vol. 6. Evidence and experience in psychiatry* (pp. 95–138). Chichester, UK: John Wiley.

Holtkamp, K., Hedebrand, J., & Herpertz-Dahlman, B. (2004). The contribution of anxiety and food restriction on physical activity in acute anorexia nervosa. *International Journal of Eating Disorders*, *36*, 163–171.

Jacobi, C., Hayward, C., de Zwaan, M., Kraemer, H.C., & Agras, W.S. (2004). Coming to terms with risk factors for eating disorders: Application of risk terminology and suggestions for a general taxonomy. *Psychological Bulletin*, *130*, 19–65.

Johnson, C. L. (1985). Initial consultation for patients with bulimia and anorexia nervosa. In D. M. Garner & P. E. Garfinkel (Eds.), Handbook of psychotherapy for anorexia and bulimia (pp. 19–51). New York: Guilford Press.

Joiner, T. E., Vohs, K. D., & Heatherton, T. F. (2000). Three studies on the factorial distinctiveness of binge eating and bulimic symptoms among non-clinical men and women. *International Journal of Eating Disorders*, *27*, 198–205.

Kaltiala-Heino, R., Rissanen, A., Rimpela, M., & Rantanen, P. (2003). Bulimia and impulsive behavior in middle adolescence. *Psychotherapy and Psychosomatics*, *72*, 26–33.

Karwautz, A., Rabe-Hesketh, S., Collier, D. A., & Treasure, J. L. (2002). Pre-morbid psychiatric morbidity, co-morbidity and personality in patients with anorexia nervosa compared to their healthy sisters. *European Eating Disorders Review, 10,* 255–270.

Katzman, M. A., & Lee, S. (1997). Beyond body image: The integration of feminist and transcultural theories in the understanding of self-starvation. *International Journal of Eating Disorders, 22,* 385–94.

Kaye, W., Devlin, B., Barbarich, N., Bulik, C. M., Thornton, L., Bacanu, S., et al. (2004). Genetic analysis of bulimia nervosa: Methods and sample description. *International Journal of Eating Disorders, 35,* 556–570.

Keys, A., Brozek, J., Henschel, A., Mickelsen, O., & Taylor, H. L. (1950). The biology of human starvation (Vols. 1–2). Minneapolis, MN: University of Minnesota Press.

Klump, K. L., & Gobrogge, K. L. (2005). A review and primer of molecular genetic studies of anorexia nervosa. *International Journal of Eating Disorders, 37,* S43–S48.

Latzer, Y., & Hochdorf, Z. (2005). A review of suicidal behavior in anorexia nervosa. *Scientific World Journal, 5,* 820–827.

le Grange, D., Gorin, A., Dymek, M., & Stone, A. (2002). Does ecological momentary assessment improve cognitive behavioral therapy for binge eating disorder? A pilot study. *European Eating Disorder Review, 10,* 316–328.

Lee H-Y., & Lock J. (2007). Anorexia nervosa in Asian-American adolescents: Do they differ from their non-Asian peers? *International Journal of Eating Disorders, 40,* 227–231.

Leitenberg, H., Rosen, J., Gross, J., Nudelman, S., & Vara, L. S. (1998). Exposure plus response-prevention treatment of bulimia nervosa. *Journal of Consulting and Clinical Psychology, 56,* 535–541.

Leon, G., Fulkerson, J. A., Perry, C., & Early-Zald, M. B. (1995). Prospective analysis of personality and behavioral vulnerabilities and gender influences in the later development of disordered eating. *Journal of Abnormal Psychology, 104,* 140–149.

Leung, N., Thomas, G., & Waller, G. (2000). The relationship between parental bonding and core beliefs in anorexic and bulimic women. *British Journal of Clinical Psychology, 39,* 205–213.

Leung, N., Waller, G., & Thomas, G. (1999). Core beliefs in anorexic and bulimic women. *Journal of Nervous and Mental Disease, 187,* 736–741.

Linehan, M. M. (1993). *Skills training manual for treating borderline personality disorder.* New York: The Guilford Press.

Lock, J., & le Grange, D. (2005). Family based treatment of eating disorders. *International Journal of Eating Disorders, 37,* S64–S67.

Lock, J., le Grange, D., Agras, W. S., & Dare, C. (2001). *Treatment manual for anorexia nervosa.* New York: The Guilford Press.

Ma, J. L. C., Chow, M. Y. M., Lee, S., & Lai, K. (2002). Family meaning of self-starvation: Themes discerned in family treatment in Hong Kong. *Journal of Family Therapy, 24,* 57–71.

Maloney, M. J., McGuire, J. B., & Daniels, S. R. (1988). Reliability testing of the children's version of the eating attitudes test. *Journal of the American Academy of Child and Adolescent Psychiatry, 27,* 541–543.

McCabe, R., McFarlane, T., Polivy, J., & Olmsted, M. P. (2001). Eating disorders, dieting, and the accuracy of self-reported weight. *International Journal of Eating Disorders, 29,* 59–64.

McFarlane, T., McCabe, R., Jarry, J., Olmsted, M. P., & Polivy, J. (2001). Weight- and shape-related self-evaluation in women with eating disorders, dieters, and non-dieters. *International Journal of Eating Disorders, 29,* 328–335.

McKay, M., & Fanning, P. (1992). *Self esteem* (2nd ed.). Oakland, CA: New Harbinger Publications Inc.

McIntosh, V. V. W., Jordan, J., Carter, F., Luty, S. E., McKenzie, J. M., Bulik, C. M., et al. (2005). Three psychotherapies for anorexia nervosa: A randomized controlled trial. *American Journal of Psychiatry, 162,* 741–747.

Meads, C., Gold, L., Burls, A., & Jobanputra, P. (1999). *In-patient versus out-patient care for eating disorders.* Birmingham, UK: University of Birmingham (DPHE Report No. 17).

Miller, W. R., & Rollnick, S. (2002). *Motivational Interviewing: Preparing people for change* (2nd ed.). New York: Guilford Press.

Mills, J., Polivy, J., Herman, C. P., & Tiggermann, M. (2002). Effects of media-portrayed idealized body images on restrained and unrestrained eaters. *Personality and Social Psychology Bulletin, 28,* 1687–1699.

Mogg, K., Bradley, B. P., Hyare, H., Lee, S. (1998). Selective attention to food-related stimuli in hunger: Are attentional biases specific to emotional and psychopathological states, or are they also found in normal drives states? *Behaviour Research and Therapy, 36,* 227–237.

Mondraty, N. K., Birmingham, C. L., Touyz, S. W., & Beumont, P. J. V. (2005). Randomised control trial for olanzopine in the treatment of cognitions in anorexia nervosa. *Australasian Psychiatry, 13,* 72–75.

Nakai, Y. (2003). The epidemiology of eating disorders: Data from Japan. In M. Maj & K. Halmi (Eds.), *Eating disorders: Vol. 6. Evidence and experience in psychiatry* (pp. 126–128). Chichester, UK: John Wiley.

National Institute for Clinical Excellence (NICE). (2004). *Eating disorders: Core interventions in the treatment and management of anorexia nervosa, bulimia nervosa and related disorders.* Clinical Guideline Number 9. London: NICE.

Nevonen, L., & Broberg, A. G. (2000). The emergence of eating disorders: An exploratory study. *European Eating Disorders Review, 8,* 279–292.

Nevonen, L., & Broberg, A. G. (2006). A comparison of sequenced individual and group psychotherapy for patients with bulimia nervosa. *International Journal of Eating Disorders, 39,* 117–127.

Nichols, D., Chater, R., & Lask, B. (2000). Children into DSM don't go: A comparison of classification systems for eating disorders in childhood and early adolescence. *International Journal of Eating Disorders, 29,* 317–324.

O'Connor, M. A., Touyz, S. W., Dunn, S., & Beumont, P. J. V. (1987). Vegetarianism in anorexia nervosa: A review of 116 consecutive cases. *Medical Journal of Australia, 147,* 540–542.

Ottosson, H., Ekselius, L., Grann, M., & Kullgren, G. (2002). Cross-system concordance of personality disorder diagnoses of DSM-IV and diagnostic criteria for research of ICD-10. *Journal of Personality Disorders, 16,* 283–292.

Pelchat, M. L. (2002). Of human bondage: Food craving, obsession, compulsion, and addiction. *Physiology and Behavior, 76,* 347–352.

Pendleton, V. R., Goodrick, G. K., Poston, W. S. C., Reeves, R. S., & Foreyt, J. P. (2002). Exercise augments the effects of cognitive-behavioral therapy in the treatment of bulimia nervosa. *International Journal of Eating Disorders, 31,* 172–184.

Pike, K. M. (2005). Assessment of anorexia nervosa. *International Journal of Eating Disorders, 37,* S22–S25.

Pike, K. M., Carter, J., & Olmsted, M. (Feb. 2005). *Cognitive behavioral therapy manual for anorexia nervosa.* (Available upon request: Kmp2@columbia.edu)

Pike, K. M., Walsh, B. T., Vitousek, K., Wilson, G. T., & Bauer, J. (2003). Cognitive behavior therapy in the post-hospitalisation treatment of anorexia nervosa. *American Journal of Psychiatry, 160,* 2046–2049.

Polivy, J. (in press). The natural course and outcome of eating disorders and obesity. In H. Klingemann & L. C. Sobell (Eds). New York: Springer.

Polivy, J., Coleman, J., & Herman, C. P. (2005). The effect of deprivation on food cravings and eating behavior in restrained and unrestrained eaters. *International Journal of Eating Disorders, 38,* 301–309.

Polivy, J., & Herman, C. P. (1987). The diagnosis and treatment of normal eating. *Journal of Consulting and Clinical Psychology, 55,* 635–644.

Polivy, J., & Herman, C. P. (1993). Etiology of binge eating: Psychological mechanisms. In C. Fairburn (Ed.), *Binge eating* (pp. 173–205). London: Guilford Press.

Polivy, J., & Herman, C. P. (2002). Causes of eating disorders. *Annual Review of Psychology, 53*, 187–213.

Polivy, J., Herman, C. P., Mills, J., & Wheeler, H. B. (2003). Eating disorders in adolescence. In G. Adams & M. Berzonsky (Eds.), *The Blackwell handbook of adolescence* (pp. 523–549). Oxford: Blackwell Publishers Ltd.

Prochaska, J. O., DiClemente, C. C., & Norcross, J. C. (1992). In search of how people change: Applications to addictive behaviors. *American Psychologist, 47*, 1102–1114.

Rieger, E., Schotte, D. E., Touyz, S. W, Beumont, P. J. V., Griffiths, R., & Russell, J. (1998). Attentional biases in eating disorders: A visual probe detection procedure. *International Journal of Eating Disorders, 23*, 199–205.

Rieger, E., Touyz, S. W., & Beumont, P. J. V. (2002). The Anorexia Nervosa Stages of Change Questionnaire (ANSOCQ). Information regarding its psychometric properties. *International Journal of Eating Disorders, 32*, 24–38.

Rieger, E., Touyz, S., Schotte, D., Beumont, P. J. V., Russell, J., Clarke, S., et al. (2000). Development of an instrument to assess readiness to recover in anorexia nervosa. *International Journal of Eating Disorders, 28*, 387–396.

Rieger, E., Wilfley, D., Stein, R. I., Marino, V., & Crow, S. J. (2005). A comparison of quality of life in obese individuals with and without binge eating disorder. *International Journal of Eating Disorders, 37*, 234–240.

Romano, S. J., Halmi, K. A., Sarkar, N. P., Koke, S. C., & Lee, J. S. (2002). A placebo-controlled study of fluoxetine in continued treatment of bulimia nervosa after successful acute fluoxetine treatment. *American Journal of Psychiatry, 159*, 96–102.

Rosen, J. C. (1997). Cognitive-behavioral body image therapy. In D. M. Garner & P. E. Garfinkel (Eds.), *Handbook of treatment for eating disorders* (2nd ed., pp. 188–201). New York: The Guilford Press.

Safer, D. L., Lively, T. J., Telch, C. F., & Agras, W. S. (2002). Predictors of relapse following successful dialectical behavior therapy for binge eating disorder. *International Journal of Eating Disorders, 32*, 155–163.

Safer, D. L., Telch, C. F., & Agras, W. S. (2001). Dialectical behavior therapy for bulimia nervosa. *American Journal of Psychiatry, 158*, 632–634.

Schlundt, D. G., & Johnson, W. G. (1990). Eating disorders: Assessment and treatment. Boston: Allyn & Bacon.

Schmidt, U. H., & Treasure, J. L. (1993). *Getting better bit(e) by bit(e): A survival kit for sufferers of bulimia nervosa and binge eating disorders.* Hove, UK: Psychology Press.

Schmidt, U. H., & Treasure, J. L. (1997). *Clinician's guide to getting better bit(e) by bit(e).* Hove, UK: Psychology Press.

Segal, Z. V., Williams, J. M. G., & Teasdale, J. D. (2002). *Mindfulness-based cognitive therapy for depression.* New York: Guilford Press.

Sobell, M. B., & Sobell, L. C. (1998). Guiding self-change. In P. Miller and G. Heather (Eds.), *Treating addictive behaviors.* (pp.189–202). New York: Plenum Press.

Soh, N., Touyz, S. W., & Surgenor, L. (2006). Eating and body image disturbances across cultures: A review. *European Eating Disorders Review, 14*, 54–65.

Spangler, D. L. (2002). Testing the cognitive model of eating disorders: The role of dysfunctional beliefs about appearance. *Behavior Therapy, 33*, 87–105.

Stice, E. (2001). A prospective test of the dual-pathway model of bulimic pathology: Mediating effects of dieting and negative affect. *Journal of Abnormal Psychology, 110*, 1–12.

Striegel-Moore, R. H. (1995) A feminist perspective on the etiology of eating disorders. In K. D. Brownell & C. G. Fairburn (Eds.), *Eating disorder and obesity. A comprehensive handbook* (pp. 224–229). New York: The Guilford Press.

Striegel-Moore, R. (1997). Risk factors for eating disorders. *Annals of the New York Academy of Sciences: Adolescent Nutritional Disorders: Prevention and Treatment, 817*, 98–109.

Striegel-Moore, R. H., Dohm, F. A., Kraemer, H. C., Schreiber, G. B., Crawford, P. B., & Daniels, S. R. (2005). Health services use in women with a history of bulimia nervosa or binge eating disorder. *International Journal of Eating Disorders, 37*, 11–18.

Striegel-Moore, R. H., Dohm, F. A., Kraemer, H. C., Taylor, C. B., Daniels. S., Crawford, P. B., & Schreiber, G. B. (2003). Eating disorders in white and black women. *American Journal of Psychiatry, 160,* 1326–1331.

Striegel-Moore, R. H., Franko, D. L., Thompson, D., Barton, B., Schreiber, G. B., & Daniels, S. R. (2005). An empirical study of the typology of bulimia nervosa and its spectrum variants. *Psychological Medicine, 35,* 1563–1572.

Strober, M. (1980). Personality and symptomatological features in young, non-chronic anorexia nervosa patients. *Journal of Psychosomatic Research, 24,* 353–359.

Sunday, S. R., Halmi, K. A., & Einhorn, A. N. (1995). The Yale-Brown-Cornell Eating Disorder Scale: A new scale to assess eating disorders symptomatology. *International Journal of Eating Disorders, 18,* 237–245.

Swinbourne, J. M., & Touyz, S. W. (2007). The co-morbidity of eating disorders and anxiety disorders: A review. *European Eating Disorders Review, 15,* 1–22.

Taylor, J., Touyz, S. W., George, L., Thornton, C., & Beumont, P. J. V. (2005). Mirror exposure as an adjunct to the treatment of anorexia nervosa: Reflecting on the data. *Proceedings of the 11th Annual Meeting of the Eating Disorder Research Society.* Toronto: Canada.

Telch, C. F., Agras, W. S., & Linehan, M. M. (2001). Dialectical behavior therapy for binge eating disorder. *Journal of Consulting and Clinical Psychology, 69,* 1061–1065.

Thornton, C., Touyz, S., & Birmingham, C. L. (2005). Eating disorders – Management in general practice. *Medicine Today, 6,* 29–34.

Touyz, S. W., & Beumont, P. J. V. (1997). Behavioral treatment to promote weight gain in anorexia nervosa. In D. M. Garner & P. E. Garfinkel (Eds), *Handbook of treatment for eating disorders* (2nd ed., pp. 361 – 371). New York: The Guilford Press.

Touyz, S. W., Beumont, P. J. V., Glaun, D., Phillips, T., & Cowie, I. (1984). A comparison of lenient and strict operant conditioning programmes in refeeding patients with anorexia nervosa. *British Journal of Psychiatry, 144,* 517–520.

Touyz, S. W., Garner, D. M., & Beumont, P. J. V. (1995). The inpatient management of the adolescent patient with anorexia nervosa. In H. C. Steinhousen (Ed.), *Eating disorders in adolescence: Anorexia and bulimia nervosa* (pp. 247–270). New York: De Gruyter/ Aldine.

Touyz, S. W., Hay, P., & Rieger, E. (in press). Eating disorders: An Australian focus. In E. Reiger (Ed), *Abnormal Psychology.* Melbourne, McGraw-Hill.

Touyz, S. W., Lennerts, W., Arthur, B., & Beumont, P. J. V. (1993). Anaerobic exercise as an adjunct to refeeding patients with anorexia nervosa: Does it compromise weight gain? *European Eating Disorders Review, 1,* 177–182.

Touyz, S. W., Lennerts, W., Freeman, R. J., & Beumont, P. J. V. (1990). To weigh or not to weigh? Frequency of weighing and rate of weight gain in patients with anorexia nervosa. *British Journal of Psychiatry, 57,* 752–754.

Touyz, S. W., Thornton, C., Rieger, E., George, L., & Beumont, P. J. V. (2003). The incorporation of the stage of change model in the day hospital treatment of patients with anorexia nervosa. *European Child and Adolescent Psychiatry, 12*(Suppl. 1), 65–71.

Treasure, J. (1997). *Anorexia nervosa: A survival guide for families, friends and sufferers.* Hove, UK: Psychology Press.

Treasure, J. L., Katzman, M., & Schmidt U. (1999) Engagement and outcome in the treatment of bulimia nervosa: First phase of a sequential design comparing motivation enhancement therapy and cognitive behavioral therapy. *Behaviour Research and Therapy, 37,* 405–418.

Treasure, J., & Schmidt, U. (2005). Anorexia nervosa. *Clinical Evidence, 13,* 1148–1157.

Treasure, J., Todd, G., Brolly, M., Tiller, J., Nehmed, A., & Denman, F. (1995). A pilot study of a randomized trial of cognitive analytical therapy vs. educational behavioral therapy for adult anorexia nervosa. *Behaviour Research and Therapy, 33,* 363–367.

Turner, H., & Bryant-Waugh, R. (2004). Eating disorder not otherwise specified (EDNOS): Profiles of clients presenting at a community eating disorder service. *European Eating Disorders Review, 12,* 18–26.

Turner, H., & Cooper, M. (2002). Cognitions and their origins in women with anorexia nervosa, normal dieters and female controls. *Clinical Psychology and Psychotherapy*, *9*, 242–252.

Van der Ham, T., Meulman, J. J., Van Strien, D. C., & van Engeland, H. (1997). Empirically based subgrouping of eating disorders in adolescents: A longitudinal perspective. *British Journal of Psychiatry*, *170*, 363–368.

Vandereycken., W., Probst, M., & van Bellinghen, M. (1992). Treating the distorted body experience of anorexia nervosa patients. *Journal of Adolescent Health*, *13*, 403–405.

Vitousek, K. B. (2002). Cognitive-behavioral therapy for anorexia nervosa. In C. G. Fairburn & K. D. Brownell (Eds.), *Eating disorders and obesity: A comprehensive handbook* (2nd ed., pp. 308–313). New York: Guilford.

Vitousek, K. B., & Hollon, S. D. (1990). The investigation of schematic content and processing in eating disorders. *Cognitive Therapy and Research*, *14*, 191–214.

Vitousek, K. B., Watson, S., & Wilson, G. T. (1998). Enhancing motivation for change in treatment resistant eating disorders. *Clinical Psychology Review*, *18*, 391–420.

Vohs, K. D., Bardone, A. M., Joiner, T. E., Abramson, L. Y., & Heatherton, T. F. (1999). Perfectionism, perceived weight status, and self-esteem interact to predict bulimic symptoms: A model of bulimic symptom development. *Journal of Abnormal Psychology*, *108*, 695–700.

Vohs, K. D., Voelz, Z. R., Pettit, J. W., Bardone, A. M., Katz, J., Abramson, L. Y., et al. (2001). Perfectionism, body dissatisfaction, and self-esteem: An interactive model of bulimic symptom development. *Journal of Social and Clinical Psychology*, *20*, 476–497.

Waller, G., Meyer, C., Ohanian, V., Elliott, P., Dickson, C., & Sellings, J. (2001). The psychopathology of bulimic women who report childhood sexual abuse: The mediating role of core beliefs. *Journal of Nervous and Mental Disease*, *189*, 700–708.

Waller, G., Ohanian, V., Meyer, C., & Osman, S. (2000). Cognitive content among bulimic women: The role of core beliefs. *International Journal of Eating Disorders*, *28*, 235–241.

Ward, A., Tiller, J., Treasure, J., & Russell, G. (2000). Eating disorders: Psyche or soma? *International Journal of Eating Disorders*, *27*, 279–287.

Ward, A., Troop, N., Todd, G., & Treasure J. (1996). To change or not to change – "How" is the question? *British Journal of Medical Psychology*, *69*,139–46.

Watkins, B., & Lask, B. (2002). Eating disorders in school-aged children. *Child and Adolescent Psychiatric Clinics of North America*, *11*, 185–200.

Wheeler, H. A., Adams, G., & Keating, L. (2001). Binge eating as a means for evading identity issues: The association between an avoidance identity style and bulimic behavior. *Identity: An International journal of Theory and Research*, *1*, 161–178.

White, M. A., Kohlmaier, J. R, Varnado-Sullivan, P., & Williamson, D. A. (2003). Racial/ethnic differences in weight concerns: Protective and risk factors for the development of eating disorders and obesity among adolescent females. *International Journal of Eating Disorders*, *8*, 20–25.

Williamson, D. A., Gleaves, D., & Stewart, T. M. (2005). Categorical versus dimensional models of eating disorders: An examination of the evidence. *International Journal of Eating Disorders*, *37*, 1–10.

Williamson, D. A., Womble, L. G., Smeets, M. A. M., Netemeyer, R. G., Thaw, J. M., Kutlesic, V., et al. (2002). Latent structure of eating disorder symptoms: A factor analytic and taxometric investigation. *American Journal of Psychiatry*, *159*, 412–418.

Wilson, G. T. (1991). The addiction model of eating disorders: A critical analysis. *Advances in Behavior Research and Therapy*, *13*, 27–72.

Wilson, G. T. (2002). Eating disorders and addictive disorders. In C. G. Fairburn & K. D. Brownell (Eds.), *Eating disorders and obesity: A comprehensive handbook* (2nd ed., pp. 199–203). New York: Guilford Press.

Windauer, U., Lennerts, W., Talbot, P., Touyz, S. W., & Beumont, P. J. V. (1993). How well are "cured" anorexia nervosa patients? An investigation of 16 weight recovered anorexia patients. *British Journal of Psychiatry*, *163*, 195–200.

Woods, S. C., & Brief, D. J. (1988). Physiological factors. In D. M. Donovan & G. A. Marlatt (Eds.), *Assessment of addictive behaviors* (pp. 296–322). New York: Guilford Press.

Wooley, S. C. (1995). Feminist influences on the treatment of eating disorders. In: K. D. Brownell & C. G. Fairburn (Eds.), *Eating disorders and obesity: A comprehensive handbook* (pp. 294–298). New York: The Guilford Press.

World Health Organization (1992). *International statistical classification of diseases and related health problems* (10th rev.). Geneva: Author.

Young, J. E., Klosko, J. S., & Weishaar, M. (2003). *Schema therapy: A practitioners guide.* New York: The Guilford Press.

# 8

# Appendices: Tools and Resources

This chapter contains the following measures and resources that therapists can copy and provide to patients:

Appendix 1:   Information Sheet for Patients – Anorexia Nervosa
Appendix 2:   Information Sheet for Patients – Bulimia Nervosa
Appendix 3:   Information Sheet for Patients – Eating Disorder Not Other Specified.
Appendix 4:   Information Sheet for Patients – Binge Eating Disorder
Appendix 5:   Checklist of Issues to Address in Therapy
Appendix 6:   Symptom Diary Record Sheet
Appendix 7:   Food Diary
Appendix 8:   A Cost-Benefit Analysis of Symptomatic Behaviors Associated with Eating Disorders
Appendix 9:   Cognitive Distortions in Eating Disorders
Appendix 10: Food Pyramid

Both the patient and her family are often struggling to obtain factual information regarding their daughter's illness. Appendices 1–4 are handouts that provide a brief explanation of the illness and can be given to those concerned. This often leads to further discussion about the nature of the illness, its treatment, and prognosis.

# Appendix 1: Information Sheet for Patients – Anorexia Nervosa

Anorexia nervosa (AN) is characterized by refusal to eat a sufficient amount to maintain a normal, healthy weight. Individuals feel fat, see themselves as fat, and are terrified of gaining weight, even when they are clearly (to others) quite underweight. In order to maintain this low body weight, those with AN attempt to restrict the type and amount of foods that they eat, often limiting their eating to a few low calorie foods that they consider "safe." They may also attempt to prevent weight gain by such means as purging (i.e., vomiting) and/or obsessive exercising. AN occurs much more often in females than in males, though males may also exhibit this problem. AN usually begins between the ages of 12 and 18, often accompanying pubertal development or a stressful life event such as changing schools. Many of the symptoms seen in these individuals are actually the result of malnutrition or starvation. These include things like feeling cold all the time, being constipated, and having lower energy levels or an inability to sit still. Psychologically, individuals with AN tend to have a need to be perfect or please others, but feel ineffective and out of control of their lives and bodies.

From: S.W. Touyz, J. Polivy, & P. Hay: *Eating Disorders*          © 2008 Hogrefe & Huber Publishers

# Appendix 2: Information Sheet for Patients – Bulimia Nervosa

Bulimia nervosa (BN) is a disorder characterized by frequent eating binges (eating a large amount of food in a short period of time) followed by attempts to compensate by getting rid of the food (e.g., by vomiting or taking laxatives), or by burning calories (excessive exercising), or by avoiding further eating for some period of time (fasting, restricting). It occurs much more often in females than in males, though males may also exhibit this problem. These individuals evaluate their self-worth based primarily on body shape and weight. If not treated, BN can result in serious medical complications including heart problems, kidney problems, digestive disorders, and even death. Individuals may also suffer from anxiety problems and depression, which also require treatment. Bulimia nervosa often begins with a diet or other weight-loss attempt that then leads to binge episodes. These may escalate into a chaotic pattern of eating characterized by food restriction/dieting, alternating with binge eating and compensatory behaviors as described above. These behaviors often produce intense feelings of guilt, disgust, and shame and individuals attempt to hide their binge eating and purging from others. This often isolates them and produces further depression.

# Appendix 3: Information Sheet for Patients – Eating Disorder Not Otherwise Specified

Eating disorder not otherwise specified (EDNOS) is not as well accepted a diagnosis as anorexia (AN) or bulimia nervosa (BN), but is more a set of residual eating disorders that don't quite meet the diagnostic criteria for AN or BN. For the most part, EDNOS refers to AN or BN without one of the key criteria (for example binge eating only one time per week rather than two or more times), or to a mixed disorder combining features of both eating disorders. Although often described as "subclinical" eating disorder, EDNOS is not necessarily less severe or distressing than AN or BN, and is actually more common than either full-blown disorder. Like AN and BN, EDNOS occurs primarily in young women, and often begins with a weight-loss diet that escalates into binge eating or severe caloric restriction. Symptoms may include binge eating and purging, or other abnormal eating behaviors such as chewing and spitting out (not swallowing) large quantities of food.

# Appendix 4: Information Sheet for Patients – Binge Eating Disorder

Binge eating disorder (BED) is one type of "eating disorder not otherwise specified," and is characterized by binge eating without the compensatory purging, fasting, or excessive exercise seen in bulimia nervosa. People with binge eating disorder have repeated binge eating episodes, eating large amounts of food quickly and secretly even when they are not hungry. As in bulimia nervosa, those with BED feel very embarrassed, depressed, distressed, or guilty about their binge eating. Although they may often attempt or think about weight control behaviors such as fasting or vomiting, they do not do these regularly, or with extreme intensity. Many of those with BED are overweight, rather than underweight. BED tends to occur more commonly in midaged women and men. This is a newer diagnostic category that is considered to be provisional at the present time until more complete data about the disorder are collected to show that this is, indeed, a valid disorder.

# Appendix 5: Checklist of Issues to Address in Therapy

**1. Weight history**
   a) Highest past weight
   b) Lowest past weight
   c) Premorbid weight and height
   d) Current weight and height

**2. Dieting/eating behaviors**
   a) History of dieting/weight control attempts
   b) Current dieting/eating pattern
   c) Binge eating
      i)   frequency
      ii)  duration
      iii) amount eaten
   d) binge foods
   e) binge triggers
   f) mood before, during, and after
   d) Inappropriate weight management behaviors (historic and current)
      i)   Fasting
      ii)  Vomiting (self-induced, substance induced, e.g., ipecac)
      iii) Diuretic/laxative abuse
      iv)  Excessive exercise

**3. Weight and shape concerns**

**4. Substance use issues**

**5. Relationship issues**
   a) Current
   b) Past (including family of origin)

**6. Mood (anxiety, depression)**

**7. Self-esteem/self-image**

**8. Identity and control issues**

**9. Personality and premorbid functioning**

**10. Treatment history**
   a) Psychological treatments
   b) Medications
   c) Hospitalizations

**11. Medical complications**

From: S.W. Touyz, J. Polivy, & P. Hay: *Eating Disorders*          © 2008 Hogrefe & Huber Publishers

# Appendix 6: Symptom Diary Record Sheet

Date:

| Symptom | Trigger | Time & Place | Thoughts | Mood Before & After |
|---------|---------|--------------|----------|---------------------|
| Binge eating | | | | |
| Vomiting | | | | |
| Laxative use | | | | |
| Diuretic use | | | | |
| Food restriction/ fasting | | | | |
| Exercising | | | | |
| Behaving to please other(s) | | | | |
| Ritualized eating (Eating in an obsessive way, e.g., cutting food into tiny pieces, or eating in a special order) | | | | |
| Weighing | | | | |
| Body checking (Looking in mirror or at reflection to check size) | | | | |

From: S.W. Touyz, J. Polivy, & P. Hay: *Eating Disorders*
© 2008 Hogrefe & Huber Publishers

# Appendix 7: Food Diary

| Time | What was eaten | Binge? | Compen-sation* | Weighing/ Body Checks | Place/ Context: (Triggers?) | Mood# |
|------|------|------|------|------|------|------|
| Morning | | | | | | |
| Midmorning | | | | | | |
| Midday | | | | | | |
| Mid-afternoon | | | | | | |
| Evening | | | | | | |
| Late evening | | | | | | |

*Vomiting/purging/exercise/fasting; # rate 0–10, 0 = *worst ever*, 10 = *best ever*; ? Behaving to please others

- Use separate sheet for each day.
- Record as close to the event as possible – at least once a day. The record may be drawn out in a diary, if desired.
- Bring the records to therapy sessions.

# Appendix 8: A Cost-Benefit Analysis of Symptomatic Behaviors Associated With Eating Disorders

S = Symptom        C = Cost        PB = Perceived benefits

## 1. S: Maintaining reduced weight

**C:** (a) Feeling cold, (b) Lack of energy, (c) Insomnia/sleep difficulties, (d) Discomfort sitting, (e) Preoccupation with food, shape, and weight (to the exclusion of normal activities and life), (f) Hair falls out, (g) Constipation, (h) Clothes don't fit properly, (i) Decreased sexual interest, (j) Dry skin, (k) Bad breath, (l) Amenorrhoea (loss of menstrual cycles and resulting infertility), (m) Osteoporosis/osteopenia (loss of bone mass resulting in fractures), (n) Potential stunting of growth.
**PB:** (a) Think they look good, (b) Reduces anxiety, (c) Gives a feeling of control, (d) Gives an identity, (e) Provides a feeling of success, (f) Gets rid of menstrual periods, (g) Feeling of power and virtuousness.

## 2. S: Binge eating

**C:** (a) Feeling out of control around food, (b) Feel compelled to perform compensatory behavior (e.g., vomiting, laxative use, diuretic use, excessive exercise, fasting), (c) Financial – cost of food, (d) Abdominal discomfort, (e) Stomach rupture, (f) Social isolation/secrecy (can't eat around other people), (g) Having to lie about missing food, (h) Embarassment about missing food and purchasing large quantities of food for a binge, (i) Shoplifting/stealing food (and getting caught).
**PB:** (a) Avoid/escape emotional issues (can't think about emotional problems when binge eating), (b) Self-soothing, (c) Takes time/alleviates boredom, (d) Get to eat foods otherwise "forbidden."

## 3. S: Vomiting

**C:** (a) Electrolyte imbalance (resulting in heart rhythm irregularities which can cause sudden death), (b) Cardiovascular irregularities, (c) Dental erosion, (d) Sores on hand and throat, (e) Having to clean bathroom, (f) Embarassment, (g) Smell (of vomit), (h) Others finding/detecting vomit, (i) Life threatening danger from emetics (e.g., ipecac).
**PB:** (a) Believe this is the way to eat and not gain weight (though in fact, calories are still absorbed and not all food is removed), (b) Tension relief, (c) Feel purified, (d) A way to upset family/express anger, (e) A means of filling "emptiness" and feeling alive.

## 4. S: Laxative abuse

**C:** (a) Severe abdominal cramps, (b) Disruption of life/schedule caused by diarrhoea, (c) Electrolyte imbalance (resulting in heart rhythm irregularities which can cause sudden death), (c) Cost of laxatives, (d) Shoplifting from pharmacy.
**PB:** (a) Belief that this gets rid of all food consumed and allows weight loss (though this is not true as calories get absorbed earlier in the digestive process), (b) Avoiding bloating or feeling full/fat, (c) Feeling empty and cleansed, (d) Relieves constipation, (e) Tension relief following bowel movement.

## 5. S: Diuretic abuse

**C:** (a) Severe electrolyte imbalance (resulting in heart rhythm irregularities which can cause sudden death), (b) Causes dehydration and dry skin, (c) Removes necessary minerals (which causes serious medical complications).
**PB:** (a) Perceived weight loss (though only very short-term).

### 6. S: Food restriction

C: (a) Can't eat favorite foods, (b) Hunger is uncomfortable, (c) Can't socialize with friends or family, (c) Arguments/conflicts about food, (d) Can't go on holidays (away from one's controlled food sources), (e) Leads to binge eating and lowered self-esteem (because one "gave in"), (f) Think about food all the time.

PB: (a) Weight loss (though frequent binges often prevent this), (b) Feeling of being in control, (c) Enjoy feeling empty, (d) Avoiding anxiety caused by food/eating, (e) Feeling of superiority (over those who eat).

### 7. S: Excessive Exercising

C: (a) Time consuming, (b) Pain and further injury when exercising despite injury, (c) Interferes with social life, (d) Fatigue, (e) Dissatisfaction that the exercise is never quite enough, (f) Behavior becomes obsessive and compelling (feel distressed if can't do same ritual every day).

PB: (a) Weight loss, (b) Feeling in control, (c) Not being lazy, (d) Feeling of superiority (over those who don't exercise as much).

### 8. S: Restless Activity

C: (a) Constantly restless/Unable to be still for even a few minutes, (b) Distressed if restricted from moving around, (c) Irritating to others.

PB: (a) Burning calories/weight loss.

### 9. S: Trying to please everyone

C: (a) Need to make others happy at own expense, (b) Frustration when this becomes impossible, (c) Increasing resentment of having to keep doing things for others, (d) Lowered self-esteem/feeling like a failure, (e) Exhaustion from working so hard to achieve increasingly unattainable goals.

PB: (a) Others will be pleased/getting love, (b) Avoiding abandonment/rejection, (c) Fear of failure.

### 10. S: Obsessive ritualized eating behaviors

C: (a) Eating becomes painfully slow and takes inordinate amounts of time, (b) Social isolation – can't eat a meal with anyone or go to restaurants, (c) Embarassing/looks strange, (d) Distressing if ritual is disturbed, (e) Gets negative attention.

PB: (a) Reduces calories consumed, (b) Reduces anxiety about eating, (c) A way to hide reduced consumption from others.

### 11. S: Frequently weighing oneself/Tyranny of the scale

C: (a) Never happy with the number – makes one miserable until next weighing, (b) Interferes with daily activities (looking for scales, refusing to go out if number was too high), (c) Emotional rollercoaster from minute fluctuations in weight, (d) Induces guilt about eating anything, (f) Different scales give different weights leading to unnecessary distress/negative mood.

PB: (a) Feel thin if weight is down (feel good, competent, etc.), (b) Need to know weight (don't trust bodies, just the scales), (c) Fear of fatness reassured by scale.

### 12. S: Body checking behaviors

C: (a) Never feel good when looking at self – destroys mood and self-esteem, (b) Becomes repetitious and obsessive, (c) Time consuming, interferes with other activities, (d) Encourages distorted perception of body.

PB: (a) Protects against getting fat (reassurance).

From: S.W. Touyz, J. Polivy, & P. Hay: *Eating Disorders*          © 2008 Hogrefe & Huber Publishers

# Appendix 9: Cognitive Distortions in Eating Disorders

1. *Body image distortion* – seeing oneself as larger than one really is. This is present in all the eating disorders, but is most prominent in AN and BN.
2. *Belief that one's weight determines one's self-worth* (higher weight = lower self-worth).
3. *Undue fear of weight gain or fatness* – applies primarily to AN and BN.
4. *Distorted beliefs about the fatteningness of foods* – leads to avoidance of carbohydrates and fats, meats (vegetarianism), and in extreme cases, vitamins, minerals, and even water. Is also associated with the belief that eating a small amount of a forbidden food, such as sugar, will lead to immediate weight gain. Many patients also believe that there are "good" and "bad" calories – a calorie of a vegetable is good, but a calorie of chocolate is bad.
5. *Believing one has binged despite eating only small or normal amounts of food* – subjective binges.
6. *Belief that once one has eaten something fattening, one is out of control and must keep eating/ bingeing* – patients give up trying to eat normally or control themselves because they believe once control is lost, it is totally gone. An associated belief is that the only way to be in control is to not eat or to eat only very limited quantities of a small range of foods.
7. *All or nothing/black or white reasoning* – thinking in an extreme fashion with no middle ground. Seeing the world and oneself in terms of acceptable or unacceptable, good or bad, worthwhile or worthless.
8. *Believing one can, and should, choose one's weight and shape regardless of one's genetic or familial physique.* The belief that one can choose the size of one's "jeans" irrespective of one's genes.
9. *Magical thinking about the importance of being under a certain weight* – e.g., under 100 pounds. Patients may believe that if they achieve an unrealistically low weight, they will be successful (at life) and if they don't, they will fail. They attribute success and failure to weight, and also extend this to other aspects of disordered eating behavior (e.g., one must take laxatives after eating anything).
10. *Extreme perfectionistic expectations* – one cannot be happy or successful at all unless one is totally perfect at everything.
11. *Belief that one can remove every calorie one has eaten by vomiting* – patients may see the stomach as maintaining food eaten in layers so that if one vomits up a food eaten early in the binge, one is getting rid of all later foods.
12. *Belief that taking laxatives and diuretics (i.e., getting rid of water) produces weight loss.*
13. *Belief that everyone is looking at one's shape and weight and judging or evaluating one based on this.* This leads to social avoidance and isolation, especially if one has eaten or feels one has binged.

From: S.W. Touyz, J. Polivy, & P. Hay: *Eating Disorders*
© 2008 Hogrefe & Huber Publishers

## Appendix 10: Food Pyramid

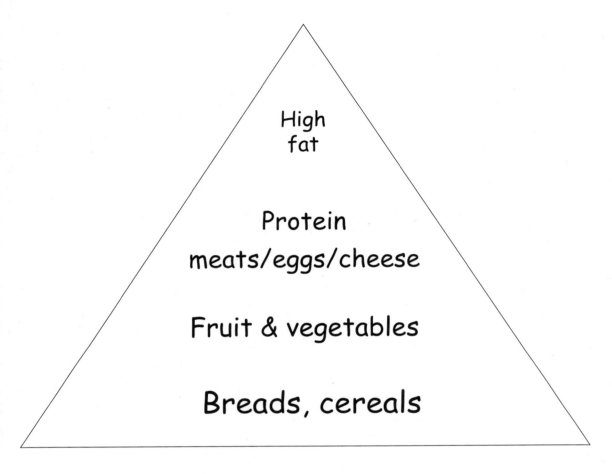

Recommended servings of each type of food group to meet basic nutritional needs:
- Breads and cereals (including potatoes, grains, etc.): 7 or more servings throughout the day
- Fruits and vegetables: 7 or more servings throughout the day
- Milk, cheese, dairy products: 3 servings per day
- Meat, eggs, nuts, and other proteins: 2 servings per day (at least one of these should contain iron)
- Foods containing fat and foods containing sugar: 3 small servings per day (approximately 1 teaspoon of butter or margarine, 1 tablespoon of olive oil, 1 teaspoon of sugar, etc.)

*Note*: It is important to maintain fluid intake of at least 6 cups of water per day, or equivalent.

For further information, see, e.g., http://www.nalusda.gov/fnic/Fpyr/pyramid.gif and recommendations from U.S. Food and Drug Administration, http://www.cfsan.fda.gov/~dms/fdpyramid.html

From: S.W. Touyz, J. Polivy, & P. Hay: *Eating Disorders*          © 2008 Hogrefe & Huber Publishers

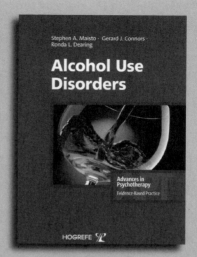

*Stephen A. Maisto, Gerard J. Connors, Ronda L. Dearing*

# Alcohol Use Disorders

### In the series: Advances in Psychotherapy – Evidence-Based Practice

2007, VIII + 94 pages, softcover, US $24.95 / € 24.95
(Series Standing Order: US $19.95 / € 19.95)
ISBN: 978-0-88937-317-4

**Practice-oriented, evidence-based guidance on treating alcohol problems – one of the most widespread health problems in modern society.**

This volume in the series *Advances in Psychotherapy – Evidence-Based Practice* provides therapists and students with practical and evidence-based guidance on the diagnosis and treatment of alcohol problems.

Alcohol abuse and alcohol dependence are widespread, and the individual and societal problems associated with these disorders have made the study and treatment of alcohol use disorders a clinical research priority. Research over the past several decades has led to the development of excellent empirically supported treatment methods. This book aims to increase clinicians' access to empirically supported interventions for alcohol use disorders, with the hope that these methods will become the standard in clinical practice.

## Table of Contents

**1. Description of Alcohol Use Disorders:** Terminology • Definition • Epidemiology • Course and Prognosis • Differential Diagnosis • Comorbidities • Diagnostic Procedures and Documentation

**2. Theories and Models of Alcohol Use Disorders:** Traditional Theories of AUDs • Biopsychosocial Model of AUDs

**3. Diagnosis and Treatment Indications:** Introduction • General Guidelines and Considerations • Drinking History • Life-Functioning • Prioritizing Problems and Needs • Referral Issues

**4. Treatment:** Introduction and Overview • Behavioral and Psychological Methods • Brief Interventions (BIs) • Extensions of Basic CBT • Psychopharmacological Methods • Mutual (Peer) Self-Help Groups • Efficacy and Prognosis • Combination of Treatment Methods • Problems in Carrying Out Treatment • Multicultural Considerations

**5. Further Reading**

**6. References**

**7. Appendix: Tools and Resources**

*"As a teacher of graduate courses on substance abuse, I have long waited for a book like this. An excellent review of evidence-based assessment and treatment methods, presented at an easily understood yet high level, objectively, and with valuable clinical advice."*
Mark B. Sobell, PhD

*"This book provides a remarkably clear, comprehensive, but succinct, coverage of our current understanding of how best to help people with alcohol use disorders. Everything the practicing clinician needs to know is there."*
Nick Heather, PhD

Order online at: **www.hogrefe.com** or call toll-free **(800) 228-3749**
please quote "APT 2008" when ordering

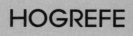 

Hogrefe & Huber Publishers · 30 Amberwood Parkway · Ashland, OH 44805
Tel: (800) 228-3749 · Fax: (419) 281-6883
Hogrefe & Huber Publishers · Rohnsweg 25 · D-37085 Göttingen
Tel: +49 551 49 609-0 · Fax: +49 551 49 609-88
E-Mail: custserv@hogrefe.com

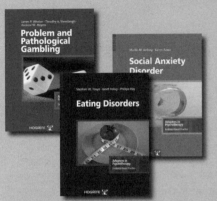
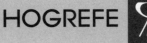